TIME TO...

DISCOVER MATHS

**Mathematical Development
in the Early Years:
How to observe, assess
and plan for progress**

TRUDI FITZHENRY
AND KAREN MURPHY

Featherstone
An imprint of Bloomsbury Publishing Plc

50 Bedford Square   1385 Broadway
London   New York
WC1B 3DP   NY 10018
UK   USA

www.bloomsbury.com

Bloomsbury is a registered trademark of Bloomsbury Publishing Plc

First published 2016

© Trudi Fitzhenry and Karen Murphy, 2016

Photography © Shutterstock/ © LEYF

British Library Cataloguing-in-Publication Data
A catalogue record for this book is available from the British Library.

ISBN:
PB 978-1-4729-1930-4
ePDF 978-1-4729-1931-1

Library of Congress Cataloging-in-Publication Data
A catalog record for this book is available from the Library of Congress.

10 9 8 7 6 5 4 3 2 1

Printed and bound in India by Replika Press Pvt Ltd.

This book is produced using paper that is made from wood grown in managed, sustainable forests. It is natural, renewable and recyclable. The logging and manufacturing processes conform to the environmental regulations of the country of origin.

With thanks to the staff and pupils at LEYF for their help with the photographs in this book.

To view more of our titles please visit www.bloomsbury.com

Contents

Introduction

This is the third book in our exciting 'Time to....' series. We hope it will prove to be a valuable and practical tool for busy practitioners.

Teaching maths with confidence has always been an area for staff development in many settings and schools. In the UK, we are generally quick to comment on how bad we think we are as mathematicians. Indeed, it appears to be culturally acceptable to share our insecurities about our mathematical abilities. However, we have a responsibility as practitioners to model confidence and competence when exploring early mathematics. This book aims to provide ideas, support and structural guidance that will enable practitioners to meet their statutory duties, which involve;

> *...providing children with opportunities to develop and improve their skills in counting, understanding and using numbers, calculating simple addition and subtraction problems; and to describe shapes, spaces, and measures.*
>
> **The Statutory Framework for the Early Years Foundation Stage 1.5**

Opening our minds to the possibilities of a world enriched by early encounters with number, shape, space and measures is the first step towards growing a new generation of intuitively confident mathematicians. Young children are born with an innate mathematical understanding and curiosity. From a very young age, children can perceive shapes and the space around them. They soon begin to organise and sort toys and objects and link daily routines to a pattern or sequence. They hear and repeat the names of numbers through sharing traditional songs, stories and rhymes. Informal learning linked to key mathematical skills and concepts occurs naturally and without explicit planning. It is our role as the adult to notice each stage of development and build on the child's emerging inquisitiveness.

Practitioners need to be able to identify the mathematics that comes out of children's self-initiated play and exploration so that they can support and extend it so that it becomes embedded learning. Some of the developmental stages contain few outcomes so it is really important for practitioners to be sure that the child is thoroughly secure in these areas and that evidence is seen across a variety of situations. For example, when completing the progress check for 16 – 26 months statement – 'Enjoys filling and emptying containers' – it may not be appropriate to tick yes if the child only ever does this at the water tray.

This book is designed for practitioners to use in settings as an assessment tool and guide as they observe, assess and support children's early mathematical skills.

How to use this book

This book supports the planning cycle at each stage of development. It contains clear guidance on what to observe, how to assess what is seen through both the assessment notes and progress checklists. Practical ideas to use in planning each child's individual next steps are also provided.

Each chapter in this book is linked to a phase or stage of development from birth to 60+ months. Each section is colour coded and links the Early Years Outcomes to the planning cycle, including observations, assessments and planning. Also included are possible links to the Characteristics of Effective Learning. Some of the photographs also contain a milestone comment. These are additional indicators of what we feel children may be able to demonstrate during this period.

There are additional activities that offer busy practitioners a wealth of ideas to choose from that are linked to that specific age and stage of development. There is a short glossary in each chapter that defines key terms as they appear. These definitions explain how we intend the words and phrases to be interpreted within the book. A traditional alphabetical glossary of all terms used appears at the back of the book for quick reference.

The progress checklists at the end of each chapter are available for practitioners to use when observing children's PSED. It is intended that the progress checklists could also be used alongside a setting's current tracking system to highlight any areas of concern and demonstrate progress made. They can be used to demonstrate progress in a specific area over time. The progress checklist at 40 – 60+ months is closely linked to the Early Learning Goal (ELG). It can be used to support the practitioner's professional judgement as to whether a child is at emerging, expected or exceeding level at the end of the Foundation Stage.

It is important that practitioners are aware of their responsibility to encourage parents to contact their health professional if the child appears to be developing outside of the normative range. If there is little or no progress after they have spoken to parents and included timed specific interventions in the child's individual plan, then practitioners should seek parental permission to involve outside agencies.

It is important that all practitioners remember that under 3s are naturally prone to putting everything and anything in their mouths as a form of sensory exploration. Practitioners must regularly check all resources and equipment available to the children to ensure they are not a choking hazard and for signs of wear, damage, sharp edges and splinters.

TIME TO DISCOVER MATH

Numbers

Early Years Outcomes

Notices changes in number of objects/images or sounds in group of up to 3.

Links to the Characteristics of Effective Learning

PLAYING AND EXPLORING

Finding out and exploring

★ showing curiosity about objects, events and people

★ using senses to explore the world around them

e.g. while lying on a changing mat the child notices the stripy socks on their feet and reaches for them. After a few attempts the socks come off and the child explores them with their mouth.

CREATING AND THINKING CRITICALLY

Making links

★ making links and noticing patterns in their experience

★ developing ideas of grouping, sequences, cause and effect

e.g. the child watches as an older child plays with a pop-up sound toy. When they leave the toy the child crawls over and tries to push the buttons that make the toy pop.

ACTIVE LEARNING

Being involved and concentrating

★ maintaining focus on their activity for a period of time

★ showing high levels of energy, fascination

★ not easily distracted

★ paying attention to details

e.g. the child is sitting supported while a practitioner blows bubbles for them to see. As they blow the bubble towards the child they count to three then pause as the child is given time to refocus on the practitioner in expectation of more bubbles. The game continues for several minutes until the child loses interest.

0 – 11 months

Observation
What you may notice...

Assessment
What it may signify...

Does the child shift their focus when the number of objects in their treasure basket changes?

▷ They may be showing an interest in the shape, texture, colour or quantity of the objects.

Do they show interest by looking at the objects when the number changes? Do they show lack of interest, by looking away, if the number of objects remains the same even though the objects may be different?

▷ They may be demonstrating a basic awareness of **cardinality**.

If you repeat two distinct sounds on a musical toy several times then only play one does the child listen or look at you for the second sound?

▷ They may be beginning to develop an awareness of pattern or sequence in sound.

Planning
What you can do...

This links to the numbers section of the Maths Progress Checklist on p17.

Providing an interesting range of objects to explore supports children's early development of number concepts. Vary the provision to include single items, pairs of items then three items. Children need to have lots of experience of pairs to be able to understand the concept of two. Sing rhymes such as *Two little pretty birds* (see p91).

Show the child two objects. If they continue to look at them remove them and then show them another two, then another two. Once the child starts to look away change to three objects and see if they bring their attention back to the objects. If they do, try adding another three. When interest wanes change the number of objects to between one and three. Stop as soon as the child appears tired (through focussing their eyes), or when they keep looking away even when the number changes.

Make up simple two and three note rhymes such as *Hello Joshua* and *1, 2, 3 sing with me* (see p91/92).

By three months old many babies are starting to demonstrate a basic awareness of cause and effect.

By 5 months, many children begin to notice changes in quantity as their awareness of different amounts develops.

Additional adult-led activities

These are additional activities or guidance to further support this stage of development.

Cardinality

Babies are born with an innate sense of cardinality. They are able to notice if the number of things they are looking at changes from as early as one week old.

What's going on?

Babies' mathematical understanding develops as they seek patterns in their play and routines. They make connections as they play with, and find out about, numbers through sorting, matching, singing number rhymes and counting.

The animals go in two by two...

Sing this well-known song and use a range of pairs of animal puppets or toys to dance in front of the child.

One, two where are your shoes?

Make time to plan for mathematical opportunities during every day routines. For example sing 'One, two where are your shoes?' (see p91) before putting shoes on.

Number 3

Sing songs and rhymes that focus on numbers up to three, such as 'One, two, three', 'Three blind mice', 'I'm coming to hug you', 'Baa, baa, black sheep' (see p91). Wherever possible use puppets or props that the child can play with to reinforce their developing understanding of number.

Home-time activities

Key communication idea

Young babies are still learning to focus their eyes and the best position for them to be able to see things is at a distance of between 20 and 36 cm.

Rhyme time

Make up rhymes and songs like 'Two little hands' (see p91) to play with baby. Remember to smile a lot, stay close and in contact, and use **caretaker speech** or **parentese**.

How many poppers?

When changing baby's clothes take the opportunity to introduce numbers and counting. For example, when undoing their sleepsuit say 'One popper pops!' then undo the popper while saying 'pop!' and looking surprised, 'Two poppers pop!' undo the next popper, continue until all poppers are undone.

When putting a sleepsuit on them count the poppers as you fasten them then when they are all done count them again, touching them gently so that the child feels and hears you counting, 'One, two, three, four poppers all done'.

Glossary of terms

Caretaker speech/parentese: a form of speech often used with babies. It can be higher in pitch than usual, has a sing-song quality and is often delivered with a smiling face, wide eyes and head movement.

Cardinality: the number of elements or objects in a group or set.

Shape, space and measures

Early Years Outcomes

Babies' early awareness of shape, space and measure grows from their sensory awareness and opportunities to observe objects and their movements, and to play and explore.

Links to the Characteristics of Effective Learning

PLAYING AND EXPLORING

Finding out and exploring

★ showing curiosity about objects, events and people

★ using senses to explore the world around them

★ showing particular interests

Being willing to 'have a go'

★ initiating activities

★ showing a 'can do' attitude

e.g. *Jack is on his tummy on the floor. He sees his favourite material blocks. He reaches out but they are too far away. He twists his body until he is in a position to wriggle backwards and get to the blocks.*

CREATING AND THINKING CRITICALLY

Making links

★ making links and noticing patterns in their experience

★ testing their ideas

★ developing ideas of grouping, sequences, cause and effect

e.g. *while sitting in a walker Tamil is playing with a rattle. He drops it to the floor then looks to see where it has gone. His **Prime Carer** retrieves it, shakes it and gives it back to him. He rattles it then drops it again. He looks to the floor, then to the adult who retrieves it again. The game continues until Tamil loses interest.*

ACTIVE LEARNING

Being involved and concentrating

★ maintaining focus on their activity for a period of time

★ showing high levels of energy, fascination

★ not easily distracted

★ paying attention to details

Keeping on trying

★ persisting with activity when challenges occur

★ showing a belief that more effort or a different approach will pay off

Enjoying achieving what they set out to do

★ showing satisfaction in meeting their own goals

★ being proud of how they accomplish something – not just the end result

e.g. *Zara is on her tummy reaching for a ball. She stretches and stretches but it is just out of reach. She looks to her **Prime carer** for help. After some encouraging smiles and **parentese** from her Prime carer, Zara stretches out her other arm as her toes push into the carpeted floor and she starts to move towards the ball. With support she is able to continue for several minutes until she reaches the ball. She smiles as she is praised for her achievement.*

Observation
What you may notice...

Assessment
What it may signify...

Does the child show an interest in different objects around them and reach for them?

The child's **visual acuity** is developing.

Does the child put all available objects in their mouth?

At birth, the mouth sensations are the most highly developed. The child may be exploring the properties of the object (such as how soft, firm or hard it is) with their mouth.

The child is fascinated by the movement of different objects and looks intently at these. They may crawl after a moving object.

The child is curious about the movement and/or object. Their **hand-eye coordination** is developing as they move towards an object they wish to grasp

Planning
What you can do...

This links to the shape, space and measure section of the Maths Progress Checklist on p17.

Encourage the child's developing sense of shape and colour by walking them around the room and chatting about the different toys and everyday objects you can see. For example, in the setting, point to the row of cushions and describe their shapes and colours.

Provide a changing selection of safe toys for the child to explore in whichever way they choose. Consider the properties and experiences the child is gaining as you choose the objects.

Play games involving rolling and moving different toys and objects towards and away from the child. Sit, with the child between your legs, opposite another practitioner and child and gently roll different coloured balls and curved shapes back and forth. If the child is ready to crawl after the object to catch it, crawl alongside them to turn it into a fun race! Describe the objects and chat about how they move and what they feel like once the child has hold of them.

At this stage children begin to judge short distances and are able to adjust their reach to pick up objects.

By 8 months some children are developing an awareness of number names and may start to use these in their speech.

Additional adult-led activities

These are additional activities or guidance to further support this stage of development.

Creative spaces

Secure **attachments** are important at this stage in supporting children to develop as confident learners. Ensure that the learning environment (both indoors and outside) supports **multi-sensory exploration** that encourages a range of physical movement at different levels and may include familiar home-linked resources. For example, create tunnels, arches, and small spaces for children to explore using cardboard boxes, plastic crates or washing baskets, sheets or tablecloths. This personal exploration of space is part of their earliest experience of the mathematical properties of **2-D** and **3-D** shapes. Provide opportunities for **heuristic** play where children are able to choose what and how they explore objects that interest them. Remember to ensure that they cannot access small objects that may be a choking hazard.

Kick and push

When the child is lying on their back (during nappy change for example) give the child opportunities to use their feet and hands to kick and push objects that provide different levels of resistance and provide **proprioceptive feedback**. For example, you could play gym with objects of different weights or by using your hands. The child will need to apply more or less pressure as you push gently on their feet causing their legs to bend then release.

Mobiles and lights

Securely position mobiles or colour-changing lights directly above a cot or mat to encourage **visual acuity** as well as arm and leg movements. Leaving a dim night light on in your child's nursery will enable them to focus on shapes and colours when awake and support their visual development. Change the position of these objects or add new shapes and colours to further stimulate interest.

Bubble fun

The child's attention will be drawn to you as you blow bubbles. They reach out to try and grab them. Continue with the game for as long as the child remains interested. Make sure you are close enough for them to be able to touch and pop some of the bubbles. If they enjoy the feeling, try blowing bubbles directly onto their hands.

Home-time activities

Key communication idea

Children instinctively start to explore their world through shape and space from the moment they are born. Initially this is by touch and exploring objects with their mouths. Encourage this exploration by offering a wide range of shapes and textures for them to hold in their mouth. Remember to ensure that they cannot access small objects that may be a choking hazard.

Bath bubbles

If the child has enjoyed the use of bubbles in the setting, extend these activities by exploring bubble bath at bath time. Talk about how the bubbles grow and cover the space as you run the taps. Let them feel the bubbles on different body parts and practise blowing them off their hands. This will help them when they want to blow bubbles with a wand.

Floating leaves

While out on a walk the child's visual attention is caught by a leaf floating past the buggy in the breeze. They follow it until it is out of sight. Describe in simple terms that a leaf is blowing in the wind. If it is not too cold allow them to feel the wind on their skin. Back in the setting, collect some coloured feathers. Blow onto the child's hand to simulate a breeze, remind them of what they saw and blow the feathers for the child. Encourage them to track the path that the feather takes with their eyes and have a go at blowing for themselves.

Glossary of terms

Prime carer: the person the child spends the most time with, e.g. a parent at home or key person in a setting.

Caretaker speech/parentese: a form of speech often used with babies. It can be higher in pitch than usual, has a sing-song quality and is often delivered with a smiling face, wide eyes and head movement.

Visual acuity: the clarity with which we see details and shapes of objects.

Hand-eye coordination: ability to use the eyes and hands together to perform an activity, for example, stringing beads, completing puzzles, playing board games.

Attachments: the affectionate tie between the child and another person.

Multi-sensory exploration: using one or more senses to explore and begin to make sense of the world around them.

Proprioceptive feedback: sensory feedback that tells us where our body is in space without having to look (e.g. being able to put an object into our mouth). It also helps us to know how much force we need to use to do something (e.g. how hard to grip something without squashing it or how to throw a ball so that it goes far enough but not too far). Activities involving resistance give us the most feedback.

2-D shape: also known as 2-dimensional. A shape that only has two dimensions (such as width and height) and no thickness.

3-D shape: also known as 3-dimensional. An object that has height, width and depth, like any object in the real world.

Heuristic play: play that allows children to initiate, make choices, explore and discover the properties and qualities of objects.

Pitch: how high or low a musical note or sound is.

Progress Checklist: 0 – 11 months

Name ....

Date						
Age in months						

Use a different coloured pen for each assessment so that progress can be seen.

Tick 'Yes' if the child consistently demonstrates this across a range of activities, indoors and outside.

Tick 'Sometimes' if the child sometimes demonstrates this, or only demonstrates it in one or two ways or situations, or usually needs adult support.

Tick 'Rarely' if the child rarely or never demonstrates this.

	Yes	Some difficulty	Severe difficulty
Numbers			
Shifts their focus when the number of objects in their treasure basket changes.			
Shows interest by looking at the objects when the number increases or decreases (if only one way state which).			
Shows lack of interest, by looking away, if the number of objects remains the same even though the objects may be different.			
If you repeat two distinct sounds on a musical toy several times then only play one does the child listen or look at you for the second sound?			
Are they more responsive to sounds of a higher or lower **pitch**? (If yes state which.)			
Shape, space and measures			
Shows an interest in different objects around them (note which ones and update these regularly as their interest changes).			
Reaches for objects of interest.			
Puts all available objects in their mouth (note if they are drawn to specific types of objects and properties).			
Is fascinated by the movement of different objects.			
Looks intently at moving objects.			
Crawls after a moving object.			

Time to Discover Maths © Trudi Fitzhenry and Karen Murphy, published by Featherstone 2016

TIME TO DISCOVER MATHS

Numbers

Early Years Outcomes

Develops an awareness of number names through their enjoyment of action rhymes and songs that relate to their experience of numbers.

Has some understanding that things exist, even when out of sight.

Links to the Characteristics of Effective Learning

PLAYING AND EXPLORING

Finding out and exploring

★ showing curiosity about objects, events and people

★ using senses to explore the world around them

★ showing particular interests

e.g. *the child approaches their* **prime carer** *with the knitted currant buns, indicating that they want them to sing the song.*

CREATING AND THINKING CRITICALLY

Making links

★ making links and noticing patterns in their experience

e.g. *playing outside in the sand, the practitioner observes the child hiding shells under a bucket. They extend the challenge by introducing first one bucket then another. Sometimes they have shells underneath, sometimes they don't. The child is fascinated by the appearance and disappearance of the shells.*

ACTIVE LEARNING

Being involved and concentrating

★ maintaining focus on their activity for a period of time

★ showing high levels of energy, fascination

e.g. *when listening to or watching nursery rhymes and songs, the child has a favourite that they react to, wanting to listen to it repeatedly. They may start to join the words or copy the actions.*

Observation
What you may notice…

The child becomes **animated** when you start to sing their favourite number songs and rhymes. They join in with some or all of the actions and say/sing the words or sounds they know that relate to the numbers.

When playing hide and seek games like Peek-a-boo! Does the child anticipate the 'boo'? Can they look for a toy that has been hidden while they were looking?

Assessment
What it may signify…

The child is beginning to **internalise** their awareness of number names aided by the repeated songs and rhymes.

The child is beginning to develop an awareness of **object permanence**.

Planning
What you can do...

This links to the numbers section of the Maths Progress Checklist on p27.

Introduce new rhymes systematically, building a bank of rhymes that are interesting and become more challenging. Remember to revisit new rhymes frequently, to support and then consolidate new learning, and older rhymes at intervals depending on children's interests.

Play a range of hide and seek games such as *Peek-a-boo one, two, three* (see p92). Play this game with up to three of the same or similar items. For example, Mr Bunny hops into view and tickles baby's tummy, hops out of sight then re-appears. Repeat this a couple of times and then make two bunnies appear. Notice any changes in reaction and repeat. Most babies will expect one bunny to appear if one tickled them, and two if there were two ticklers. Alternate between one and two, giving the child a couple of goes to adapt to the new number. When you are confident that the child is able to notice the difference you may want to try adding a third.

During this stage most children have developed some sense of **object permanence.**

During this stage some children may start to use a few number names as they attempt to join in a familiar rhymes. They may not yet have an understanding of the corresponding quantity.

Additional adult-led activities

These are additional activities or guidance to further support this stage of development.

Make sure you have a varied **repertoire** of number songs and rhymes that include counting forwards and backwards, the words 'no' or 'none', and counting to five then ten.

Number songs and rhymes

'Three jelly fish', 'Five little speckled frogs', 'Five currant buns', 'Five fat sausages', 'Five little firefighters'.

Wherever possible use puppets and/or props which the child can hold or use. If these are numbered it will also support both ordering and number recognition. Remember to make the puppets and/or props available during free-flow play for children to practise and embed their learning.

Where's she gone?

When dressing or undressing the child and pulling their clothes over their head, say 'Where's she gone?' in a sing-song voice and look surprised when the child reappears.

Home-time activities

Key communication idea

Use opportunities in daily life, such as putting away the shopping, to introduce numbers. As they listen to you counting the cans of beans into the cupboard they experience mathematics in a real and practical way.

Copy me

Whenever you have time together where you are waiting for something, such as a bus or health check, use the time to make up copy cat rhymes like this:

One, two, three can you copy me?

Can you copy me and clap?

One, two, three can you copy me?

Can you copy me and wave?

Extend the activity to include a range of actions and directions. For example,

Can you copy me and clap up high?

Can you copy me and wave to the right? (remembering to mirror so that the child copies in the right direction for them)

As confidence grows add in a child's name and let them choose the action.

Glossary of terms

Internalise: absorb learning at a deeper level.

Object permanence: understanding that things continue to exist even when they cannot be seen, heard, touched, smelled or sensed.

Repertoire: a stock of words, songs and rhymes that are regularly used.

Animated: lively and with action.

Shape, space and measures

Early Years Outcomes

Recognises big things and small things in meaningful contexts.

Gets to know and enjoy daily routines, such as getting-up time, mealtimes, nappy time and bedtime.

Links to the Characteristics of Effective Learning

PLAYING AND EXPLORING

Finding out and exploring

★ showing curiosity about objects, events and people

★ using senses to explore the world around them

★ engaging in open-ended activity

★ showing particular interests

Being willing to 'have a go'

★ initiating activities

★ taking a risk, engaging in new experiences, and learning by trial and error

e.g. Tommy is playing with a selection of hair accessories which includes a large and a small brush, comb, hair clip and toggle. When he gets to the large brush he looks at it, mouths the bristles then holds it out to his **Prime carer** who uses it to brush their own, then Tommy's hair, **commentating** as he does so. He hands it back to Tommy, leaning in so that Tommy can have a go at brushing.

ACTIVE LEARNING

Being involved and concentrating

★ showing high levels of energy, fascination

★ not easily distracted

★ paying attention to details

CREATING AND THINKING CRITICALLY

Having their own ideas

★ thinking of ideas

★ finding new ways to do things

e.g. Anton is exploring some new sound toys. He uses mouthing, handling, shaking and banging to discover all he can about the properties of the new toys. As his interest wanes a practitioner shows him how to make new noises and new actions happen and he continues to explore.

Observation
What you may notice...

Can the child select objects by size when requested? For example, can the child select the correct ball if asked to roll the big ball to a practitioner, then the little ball from a selection of two.

Assessment
What it may signify...

The child is developing an awareness of size.

Can the child identify familiar items from a selection of objects used at snack time? For example a cup, a plate, a bowl or a spoon. Do they bang the spoon excitedly on the bowl while waiting for their food?

The child is familiar with, and starting to anticipate the next event in a particular routine.

Planning

What you can do...

This links to the shape, space and measures section of the Maths Progress Checklist on p27.

Provide children with a simple choice between two things, such as a thick chunky paintbrush or a longer thinner one. **Commentate** as the child chooses and uses the item. For example, at the dough table there is a large piece of dough and a much smaller one. The child chooses the large piece. The adult says 'I see you've chosen the big lump of dough. I'll use the little lump.' The adult continues to **commentate** as the child plays, making frequent reference to size and comparing their pieces of dough.

Ensure that all practitioners follow the same pattern with routines such as snack time, nappy change, home-time. For example, if the setting has a goodbye song or sign that is sung or used before coats are put on to go home all practitioners need to be consistent with how and when they use it.

Note ways in which the child demonstrates their developing understanding of time passing or of past and future events. Clarify any misunderstandings and model the correct use of tenses when responding.

Singing rhymes relating to the child's daily routines and familiar objects helps to consolidate and embed learning about shape and time.

Additional adult-led activities

These are additional activities or guidance to further support this stage of development.

Now I'm little, now I'm big

Collect a range of materials that can change shape and size easily, such a scarves, lycra, sponges, a blow-up beach ball. As you say 'Now I'm little' make the object as small as possible. As you say 'Now I'm big' open it out, stretch it, allow it to expand or blow it up. Then reverse the process. Vary the volume and speed of your speech to create anticipation and interest.

Teddy Bear, Teddy Bear

Play movement games that encourage changing body shape and position such as 'Teddy Bear, Teddy Bear' (see p92).

Music time – select particular tunes or pieces of music that will be used daily to signify different times and events. For example, a lively tidy-up time song, a calming lullaby to help when resting, a welcome song to start the day.

Home-time activities

Key communication idea

Encourage parents/carers to share what they notice about the child's awareness of routine events at home. Tell them about any new ways in which the child has anticipated or linked parts of a routine. For example, if the child collects a beaker when they hear the music that is played during snack time. If the setting sends home a diary/book, short comments can be included which will provide a running record of how this is developing over time.

Story time

Read simple board books and bath books that focus on big and little to reinforce the understanding the children are developing of shape and space through their **heuristic** and **multi-sensory play**.

Glossary of terms

Prime carer: the person the child spends most time with e.g. parent at home or key person/paired key person or buddy in a setting.

Commentating: speaking out loud about what you notice the child doing while you play alongside them. This provides them with new vocabulary and models correct speech.

Heuristic play: play that allows children to initiate, make choices, explore and discover the properties and qualities of objects.

Multi-sensory exploration: using one or more senses to explore and begin to make sense of the world around them.

Progress Checklist: 8 – 20 months

Name ....

Date					
Age in months					

Use a different coloured pen for each assessment so that progress can be seen.

Tick 'Yes' if the child consistently demonstrates this across a range of activities, indoors and outside.

Tick 'Sometimes' if the child sometimes demonstrates this, or only demonstrates it in one or two ways or situations, or usually needs adult support.

Tick 'Rarely' if the child rarely or never demonstrates this.

	Yes	Some difficulty	Severe difficulty
Numbers			
Becomes **animated** when you start to sing their favourite number songs and rhymes (note favourites, updating these as they change).			
Joins in some or all of the actions and says/sings the words or sounds they know that relate to the numbers (note and track which numbers they use).			
Enjoys playing hide and seek games like Peek-a-boo!			
Anticipates the 'boo'.			
Looks for a toy that they have watched being hidden.			
Managing feelings and behaviour			
The child seeks out their prime carer in response to a range of experiences in order to share their emotions and have these validated.			
The child may suck their thumb or show other signs of needing comfort through accessing a regular relaxation area or familiar comfort object. (Note favourites.)			
The child joins in with some care giving routines. (Note which ones.)			
When the child is asked to do or not to do something, they often comply.			
Space, shape and measures			
Selects an object by size from a selection of two same objects.			
Selects an object by size when requested from a group (if this is limited note which objects the child responds to best , for example, balls, teddies, trucks).			
Anticipates aspects of a regular routine. For example, banging the spoon excitedly on the bowl while waiting for their food.			
Selects familiar objects to use as part of a regular routine. For example, a coat or shoes before going outside (not necessarily their own).			

Welcome to Discover Maths © Trudi Fitzhenry and Karen Murphy, published by Featherstone 2016

Numbers

Early Years Outcomes

Knows that things exist, even when out of sight.

Beginning to organise and categorise objects, e.g. putting all the teddy bears together or teddies and cars in separate piles.

Says some counting words randomly.

Links to the Characteristics of Effective Learning

PLAYING AND EXPLORING

Finding out and exploring

★ showing curiosity about objects, events and people

★ using senses to explore the world around them

★ engaging in open-ended activities

★ showing particular interests

Being willing to 'have a go'

★ initiating activities

★ showing a 'can do' attitude

e.g. *Joey's* **prime carer** *notices that as soon as he arrives in the setting he goes over to the construction area. He looks at the available materials then starts to play with them. Sometimes building, sometimes just exploring their textures and properties, spinning wheels or moving items around.*

ACTIVE LEARNING

Being involved and concentrating

★ showing high levels of energy, fascination

★ paying attention to details

Enjoying achieving what they set out to do

★ enjoying meeting challenges for their own sake rather than external rewards or praise

e.g. *after playing peek-a-boo with his key person, Ali continues to hide objects under the blanket. He says 'Where car gone?' and laughs to himself as he lifts the blanket. The game continues for several minutes.*

CREATING AND THINKING CRITICALLY

Having their own ideas

★ thinking of ideas

Making links

★ making links and noticing patterns in their experience

e.g. *Sophie notices one of the adults is changing their shoes and putting their coat on. She thinks this means it will soon be time to go outside so she goes to find some wellies. She returns with some boots and places them on the floor.*

16 – 26 months

Observation
What you may notice...

Assessment
What it may signify...

Does the child look for favourite toys in familiar places and seek support to find them when they are not there? For example, when playing with the wooden trains Zac looks for the blue Thomas engine. When he can't find it he tugs at an adult's arm and says 'Thomas gone!'

The child has some understanding of **object permanence**.

Does the child sometimes appear to sort or group objects during independent play? For example, the child selects all of the play figures from the construction set.

The child is showing an awareness of sorting objects based on their interests and needs.

Does the child sometimes use number names spontaneously during independent play? For example, when playing with big bricks, while stacking or lining them up the child says 'two' then continues playing.

The child is beginning to show an interest in number and repeats known number names in an appropriate context.

Planning
What you can do...

This links to the numbers section of the Maths Progress Checklist on p37.

Continue playing hide-and-seek games, involving the child in some of the hiding.

Encourage the child to talk about family members or pets, being aware not to make them anxious about being apart from them.

Children will enjoy playing 'feely bag' games and discovering different shapes and objects whilst you describe and name them.

Use tidy-up time as an opportunity to encourage children to match and sort objects. You can set challenges such as finding all the animals and putting them in their tray before the glitter bottle or music track runs out.

Join in with the child's play counting to three as you stack or line up three bricks. Repeat the process if the child is happy for you to be playing alongside or they appear interested in what you are doing. Increase the numbers in order if the child is interested.

Some children may be starting to identify pairs of items as two, and three or more as many.

Additional adult-led activities

These are additional activities or guidance to further support this stage of development.

Children for whom English is an additional language may already have knowledge of number in their first/home language. Discuss with parents how you can support them while introducing them to English. Parents may be able to teach the children or practitioners some number songs and rhymes that they use at home or record them for sharing within the setting.

Essential activities

Matching, sorting, pairing (**one-to-one correspondence**) and ordering are essential to developing an understanding of mathematics. Try to ensure that children are given opportunities daily to engage in interesting and playful activities in each of these areas. At times these can be adult-led, such as setting a challenge that involves one or more activities. For example, ask the child to find all the fir cones in a basket of cones, conkers and shells (matching). Then ask them to put the big ones together and the small ones together (sorting), if they are still interested next ask them to give each teddy a cone (pairing). Provide collections of objects that children can sort freely (change these regularly so that they contain new and unusual items). Practitioners can play alongside and use relevant mathematical vocabulary in a meaningful context and at an appropriate level to support the child to express their ideas.

Home-time activities

Key communication idea

Object permanence is a precursor to the symbolic understanding necessary for mathematical development. Parents can support this by talking to babies and young children when they are nearby but out of sight. This also reassures children who may be become anxious about being apart from their **prime carer**.

Now you see it!

A peek-a-boo variation. Pull a small scarf or piece of silky material through a kitchen roll tube. Let the child see the scarf going in, pause once it is completely hidden, show the child the tube (covering the ends with your hands) and say 'Oh no! Where's it gone?', then pull the scarf out of the other end and say 'Wow! It's back again!'.

Touching, listening and looking walks

Young children categorise, or sort, objects in their attempts to make sense of their world. When out for a walk to the park, the shops or even just to the car spend some time focusing on sights, sounds and textures. For example, gently rub their hands over a bumpy tree trunk or a smooth railing. Crumble a dry leaf near their ear or stop and listen to any nearby sounds. Point out planes or birds flying overhead. Use simple language to describe each experience and let the child participate physically as much as it is safe to do so.

Glossary of terms

One-to-one correspondence: being able to point to an individual object while counting and matching a number to each object.

Object permanence: understanding that things continue to exist even when they cannot be seen, heard, touched, smelled or sensed.

Commentating: speaking out loud about what you notice the child doing while you play alongside them. This provides them with new vocabulary and models correct speech.

Prime carer: the person the child spends most time with e.g. a parent at home or key person in a setting

Shape, space and measures

Early Years Outcomes

Attempts, sometimes successfully, to fit shapes into spaces on inset boards or jigsaw puzzles.

Uses blocks to create their own simple structures and arrangements.

Enjoys filling and emptying containers.

Associates a sequence of actions with daily routines.

Beginning to understand that things might happen 'now'.

Links to the Characteristics of Effective Learning

PLAYING AND EXPLORING

Finding out and exploring

★ showing curiosity about objects, events and people

★ using senses to explore the world around them

★ engaging in open-ended activity

★ showing particular interests

Being willing to 'have a go'

★ initiating activities

★ seeking challenge

★ showing a 'can do' attitude

★ taking a risk, engaging in new experiences, and learning by trial and error

e.g. Ali is outside exploring the new mud kitchen. While his friends fill pots and make 'lunch' he tries, unsuccessfully, to squeeze himself behind the wooden structure, then crawls under it using it as a den.

ACTIVE LEARNING

Being involved and concentrating

★ maintaining focus on their activity for a period of time

★ showing high levels of energy, fascination

★ not easily distracted

★ paying attention to details

Keeping on trying

★ persisting with an activity when challenges occur

Enjoying achieving what they set out to do

★ showing satisfaction in meeting own goals

★ enjoying meeting challenges for their own sake rather than external rewards or praise

e.g. Ollie is drawn to the new floor puzzle. He quickly finds two pieces that fit together. He tries two more pieces, turning them round to see if they will fit. They don't. He tries another, but still cannot find the piece he needs. He looks to a practitioner for support. They show him the box and help him to complete the puzzle. Ollie looks at the completed puzzle for a few seconds then goes off to another activity.

CREATING AND THINKING CRITICALLY

Having their own ideas

★ thinking of ideas

★ finding ways to solve problems

★ finding new ways to do things

e.g. Alice and May are playing with the wooden train set. May moves her train slowly and Alice keeps crashing into her. With practitioner support they are able to develop the simple circular track to include junctions and bridges so that they can play at their own pace without collisions.

16 – 26 months

Observation
What you may notice...

Can the child complete a simple four piece peg puzzle?

Does the child manipulate large soft play shapes to create structures of their own?

Does the child spend time filling and emptying containers? For example, at the sand or water tray.

Does the child anticipate mealtimes when they see the table being set or highchairs being brought in? Do they sometimes go towards the sink in readiness for hand washing?

Does the child take a coat to a practitioner if they want to go outside?

Assessment
What it may signify...

Their **hand-eye coordination** is developing as well as their awareness of shape and size.

They are developing an awareness of the properties of shapes and how they may fit together and balance.

The child is starting to learn about **volume** and is exploring concepts such as full and empty. They may be developing their problem-solving skills. For example, how to fill a bucket with a hole in it.

The child is able to connect a series of events from a daily routine.

The child is able to associate an action with an event that they want to happen at the present time.

Planning
What you can do...

This links to the shape, space and measures section of the Maths Progress Checklist on p37.

Provide a selection of shape sorters and puzzles of increasing difficulty. Ensure that these have all the pieces and are complete.

Offer different shaped and sized objects for stacking and building. Make sure that some have a curved surface for challenge.

Set out pots, pans and pebbles of varying sizes. Introduce language such as 'full' and 'empty', 'heavy' and 'light'. Play games at tidy-up time that involve filling boxes with toys as quickly as possible.

Ensure that familiar routines follow a consistent pattern. It may be beneficial for children for whom English is an additional language or who may have additional needs to use a timeline when establishing new routines or any changes to routines.

Talk to the child about cause and effect during routines. For example, 'I am putting the plates on the table as we are going to have our snack now'.'

By 24 months many children are able to complete simple insert or peg puzzles.

16 – 26 months

Additional adult-led activities

These are additional activities or guidance to further support this stage of development.

Mathematical language

Practitioners need to value and encourage children's attempts to use mathematical language in their play. It is important to gradually introduce vocabulary concerning shape, space, position, movement, direction, pattern and measurement in ways that are meaningful and make sense to the child. The actual name of a shape or colour of an object is far less important than hands-on exploratory experiences that support problem-solving, matching skills and the acquisition of useful descriptive language.

Explorers

To continue to support children's developing awareness of space, direction and distance involve them in setting up more challenging areas to explore that allow them to crawl inside, through and around, climb up, down and over.

Home-time activities

Key communication idea

A child develops much of their understanding of the world around them through trial and error. At this stage many enjoy posting objects into any space they find. Support their curiosity by making post boxes out of cereal boxes or shoeboxes. Cut out a selection of holes of varying shapes and sizes and help them to post everyday objects. When they lose interest in the posting show them how you open the box and put the objects away together.

What, where and when

As the child starts to experiment with language note any that relates to size, shape, position or sequence of events. When out for a walk, in the car, on a bus, a train or in the garden take time to draw the child's attention to objects and events of interest. This will help them to extend their vocabulary and understanding. Where possible, use short sentences. Try playing 'One, two, three, what can we see?' (p.91)

Glossary of terms

Hand-eye coordination: ability to use the eyes and hands together to perform an activity, for example, stringing beads, completing puzzles, playing board games.

Volume: the amount of space filled by an obje‑ or substance, or the amount of space inside a container.

Progress Checklist: 16 – 26 months

Name ....

Date						
Age in months						

Use a different coloured pen for each assessment so that progress can be seen.

Tick 'Yes' if the child consistently demonstrates this across a range of activities, indoors and outside.

Tick 'Sometimes' if the child sometimes demonstrates this, or only demonstrates it in one or two ways or situations, or usually needs adult support.

Tick 'Rarely' if the child rarely or never demonstrates this.

	Yes	Some difficulty	Severe difficulty
Numbers			
Looks for favourite toys in familiar places.			
Seeks adult support to find them when they are not there (note adult/s the child goes to frequently).			
Sometimes appears to sort or group objects during independent play (note particular favourites and monitor as this changes).			
Sometimes uses number names spontaneously during independent play (note which ones and the context in which they are used).			
Space, shape and measures			
Completes a simple four piece peg puzzle. (If 'Yes' note other types and size of puzzle the child completes regularly.)			
Manipulates large soft play shapes to create structures of their own.			
Manipulates smaller blocks to create structures of their own (note any favourites and repeated designs).			
Spends time filling and emptying containers (note which areas they access to do this).			
Anticipates some actions linked to familiar routines (note which routines).			
Shows some understanding that things might happen now. For example, the child takes a coat to a practitioner when they want to go outside.			

Time to Discover Maths © Trudi Fitzhenry and Karen Murphy, published by Featherstone 2016

TIME TO DISCOVER MATH

Numbers

Early Years Outcomes

Selects a number of objects from a group when asked, for example, *'please give me one'*, *'please give me two*.

Recites some number names in sequence.

Creates and experiments with symbols and marks representing ideas of number.

Begins to make comparisons between quantities.

Uses some language of quantities, such as *'more'* and *'a lot'*.

Knows that a group of things changes in quantity when something is added or taken away.

Links to the Characteristics of Effective Learning

PLAYING AND EXPLORING

Finding out and exploring

★ showing curiosity about objects, events and people

★ using senses to explore the world around them

★ engaging in open-ended activity

Being willing to 'have a go'

★ initiating activities

★ seeking challenge

e.g. *Delilah and Bradley are outside collecting objects for their outdoor maths classroom. Bradley returns with some twigs, leaves and conkers. He stacks his twigs and leaves to make a nest for his conkers. Delilah watches and attempts to create her own nest. She asks Bradley to share his conkers because he has got more.*

CREATING AND THINKING CRITICALLY

Having their own ideas

★ thinking of ideas

★ finding ways to solve problems

★ finding new ways to do things

Making links

★ making links and noticing patterns in their experience

Choosing ways to do things

★ planning, making decisions about how to approach a task, solve a problem and reach a goal

e.g. *Sarah is playing with the garage set. Using sticky notes she draws a squiggle then sticks it onto a parking space. She parks the car and says 'Like the bikes outside'.*

ACTIVE LEARNING

Being involved and concentrating

★ showing high levels of energy, fascination

★ paying attention to details

Enjoying achieving what they set out to do

★ showing satisfaction in meeting their own goals

★ being proud of how they accomplished something – not just the end result

Observation
What you may notice...

Assessment
What it may signify...

Can the child count a given number of objects into the practitioner's hand one at a time?

The child is becoming aware of **one-to-one correspondence**.

Does the child sometimes recite numbers in their play? For example while building a tall tower the child touches each brick and says 'One, two, three, four, one, two, three, four, one two' etc.

The child wants to count the bricks but is only currently familiar with counting to four so repeats known numbers until all cars have been counted.

Does the child choose to mark make their own 'numbers' during play?

The child is showing an interest in **mathematical graphics**. The child chooses how to represent their ideas in a way that is meaningful to them.

Can the child make some comparison of **quantity**? For example, when playing with the large construction toys Abbie starts to grab some wheels from another child. As a practitioner intervenes to support a resolution Abbie says 'she got more'.

The child has some awareness of **quantity**, particularly when it is relevant to their needs.

Does the child sometimes use language relating to **quantity** appropriately in their play?

The child has a developing understanding of **quantity** and is starting to recognise 'more' and 'less'.

Does the child understand that if someone adds another carriage to the train there are now more carriages?

Does the child understand that if someone takes a carriage from the train there are now less carriages?

The child is beginning to gain an understanding of the concepts of addition and subtraction.

Planning
What you can do...

This links to the number section of the Maths Progress Checklist on p47.

Include counting out activities in daily routines. For example, when preparing for outdoor play count wellies and gloves as they are put on e.g. 'One welly, two wellies … now you count your gloves …' Extend the child's counting skills by counting and naming all of the items they have put on together as they dressed.

Praise the child's attempt rather than correcting them and risking putting them off counting. Provide plenty of opportunities for counting together throughout the next and subsequent days.

Encourage children to develop their own **mathematical graphics** by modelling these across a wide range of contexts. For example, make a tally of children going out for a walk while doing the head count and show the children how it can be used to check everybody is back safely.

Provide practical opportunities for comparisons. For example, shell broad beans that you have grown together. Open two pods, lay them side by side. Count the number of beans in each and compare sizes. Introduce vocabulary such as more, less, bigger and smaller.

By 3 years old many children can count up to 4 objects. Counting at this stage is more of a recital of numbers in sequence than an understanding of quantity.

Support opportunities for sharing while counting. For example, sharing dough cookies that they have made with the teddies. Encourage use of mathematical language such as more, less, a lot, a little.

Play games and sing songs that involve counting forwards and backwards. For example, snakes and ladders, target games and the How many children song (see songs and rhymes p92).

Additional adult-led activities

These are additional activities or guidance to further support this stage of development.

Mathematical graphics

It is important to show the child that all attempts at mathematical representation are valued by creating a culture within the setting which encourages all forms of **graphical representation**. These may include scribbling, drawing, writing, tallying, recognisable numbers and the child's own symbols. Note the contexts in which each child attempts representation in order to provide additional interesting opportunities that will further encourage this and allow the practitioner to support the child's mathematical understanding by building on what they already know and like. Share these with parents, explaining their relevance and how this type of representation supports their child's developing ability to problem solve.

Mathematical hotspots

It is essential that interesting practical opportunities are available on a regular basis within small-group activities and throughout the play environment to encourage exploration and collaborative dialogue that includes mathematical discussion. Provide varied equipment such as raffle books, large calculators, clipboards, number sponges, counting beads and natural resources. Ensure that any interests shown by the children are supported where appropriate and developed to consolidate learning and move to the next level of learning.

Ten trucks song

Sing this song while playing with a wooden train set, or adapt it to other vehicles such as cars, planes or diggers. See songs and rhymes on p93.

Home-time activities

Key communication idea

Supporting children to recognise number in their everyday routines helps them to consolidate their learning. For example, count socks in pairs as they go into the washing machine then do this again while the child matches them as they are taken out and pegged on a line or airer.

Ready for bed

Make up counting rhymes to say at bedtime. For example, gather the child's favourite soft toys or teddies to put away at bedtime. As the first toy is put away say 'One toy ready for bed'. Then as the next toy joins it 'Two toys ready for bed'. Continue until all the toys are away then finally count them all one more time and say goodnight to them all.

Counting sheep

See songs and rhymes on p92.

Glossary of terms

One-to-one correspondence: being able to point to an individual object while counting and matching a number to each object.

Mathematical graphics: the marks and representations used by children to express their mathematical thoughts. The child chooses how to represent their ideas in a way that is meaningful to them.

Shape, space and measures

Early Years Outcomes

Notices simple patterns and shapes in pictures.

Beginning to categorise objects according to properties such as shape or size.

Begins to use the language of size.

Understands some talk about immediate past and future, e.g. 'before', 'later', or 'soon'.

Anticipates specific time-based events such as mealtimes or home-time.

Links to the Characteristics of Effective Learning

PLAYING AND EXPLORING

Playing with what they know

★ taking on a role in their play

★ acting out experiences with other people

Being willing to 'have a go'

★ showing a 'can do' attitude

ACTIVE LEARNING

Being involved and concentrating

★ maintaining focus for a period of time

★ paying attention to details

Keeping on trying

★ persisting with activity when challenges occur

★ believing that more effort pays off

★ bouncing back after difficulties

Enjoying achieving what they set out to do

★ showing satisfaction in meeting own goals

★ enjoying meeting challenges for their own sake rather than external rewards or praise

CREATING AND THINKING CRITICALLY

Having their own ideas

★ finding ways to solve problems

★ finding new ways to do things

Making links

★ testing their ideas

Choosing ways to do things

★ making decisions about how to approach a task, solve a problem and reach a goal

★ changing strategy as needed

e.g. Jay and Kara are playing in the shop. Jay selects a number of tins of produce, pays and waits as Kara tries to pack them into the small plastic basket. They won't all fit and the handle comes off as Jay picks it up. Together they decide they need a bigger and stronger basket. They try other bags and boxes but they are all too small or not strong enough. Kara has an idea. She rushes outside and returns with a pull-along trolley. Together they load it and Kara helps Jay pull it to his car outside. She smiles at Jay saying 'Now you can go home'.

22 – 36 months

Observation	Assessment
What you may notice...	**What it may signify...**

Can the child point to simple shapes and patterns when prompted?

The child's **visual acuity** and **discrimination** are developing.

Does the child sometimes sort objects according to properties of their own choosing? For example: buttons by colour, dinosaurs by size or play food by 'nice' and 'nasty'.

The child is beginning to **categorise**.

Is the child beginning to use the language of size in their self-initiated play?

The child is developing an awareness of size in a meaningful context.

Does the child sometimes use language relating to their immediate past or future? For example, 'Me had/have birthday' when they bring some cake into the setting the day after their birthday.

The child is beginning to understand the concept of time passing. That some things have already happened and that some are yet to happen.

Does the child anticipate some time-based events?

The child is developing an understanding of **cause and effect**.

Planning
What you can do...

This links to the shape, space and measures section of the Maths Progress Checklist on p47.

Make large 'spot the difference' cards. Include colour on some to highlight difference in shapes, size and position.

Play 'feely bag pairs'. Collect a selection of pairs of objects. Put one set in a feely bag. Let the child see and feel one of the objects while you describe its properties. The child then has to feel inside the bag and try to find the matching object. Start with objects that are very different such as hard plastic building blocks, soft teddies, rubber balls and some cups.

Make big and little lotto games where the child has to match not only the object but the correct size. Collect pairs of doll and baby socks in different sizes. Ask the child to match the socks to a doll or teddy. The biggest pair on the biggest feet. Model language such as small, smaller and smallest.

Use large sand-timers to help with turn taking, understanding passage of time and future events. Ensure that the timers are able to run for one or two minutes initially as even this may seem like a very long time to the child. Increase the length of time as the child's concentration and understanding develop.

All practitioners need to be consistent in how they follow regular routines. For example, singing the tidy-up song means that at the end of the song we all stop what we are doing and help to tidy.

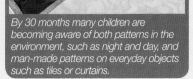

By 30 months many children are becoming aware of both patterns in the environment, such as night and day, and man-made patterns on everyday objects such as tiles or curtains.

Additional adult-led activities

These are additional activities or guidance to further support this stage of development.

Traditional songs

Many traditional stories can be used to consolidate the outcomes at this stage. For example sing 'When Goldilocks went to the house of the bears' (p93) – use puppets to tell the story, props for matching, and provide outfits for dressing up and role play.

Let's wrap

Collect a selection of wrapping paper that includes repeating patterns or distinct objects and shapes that can be used to make a variety of games. For example: pattern making where the child continues the pattern by selecting a pre-cut matching pattern, or makes their own repeating pattern from individual shapes. Also make matching pairs, lotto, and 'spot the difference' activities.

Water levels

Support children's developing understanding of capacity by drawing their attention to what happens to the level of water or milk as drinks are poured at snack or meal times. Mark the level of liquid on the side of the jug then, as each child pours (or is supported with pouring), talk about what is happening and mark the new level on the jug. Children may also like to compare amounts in their cups. You can also talk about weight. The jug may be too heavy for the first child to hold but by the second or third it may be possible for them to hold and pour independently. The children may think one child is stronger so as the jug gets lighter let them all feel the weight and practise pouring.

Home-time activities

Key communication idea

Being able to recognise patterns is a crucial skill for later learning. To do this children need to be able to see differences. Support them with this through the types of games mentioned and by drawing their attention to changes in their environment. For example, when it gets dark early in the winter and the lights need to be switched on. Model appropriate language for them to link to the idea or objects.

Wash day sort

Ask the child to help sort the washing as you put it onto the line or airer. You can sort by item (e.g. all the pants together), by colour, by size (e.g. big T-shirts, little ones) or pattern (e.g. anything with spots together).

I-See

A simple version of 'I-spy' to develop observation skills. Start with familiar objects. For example, 'I see, and it's clear to me, I can see a big brown teddy. Can you bring it to me?'. Praise the child's efforts and when they are confident with the game encourage them to 'see' things for you to find.

Glossary of terms

Visual acuity: the clarity with which we see details and shapes of objects.

Visual discrimination: distinguishing similarities and differences between shapes and objects.

Categorise: to put or sort things that have some similar or same features into a group.

Cause and effect: when something (the cause) makes something else happen (the effect).

Progress Checklist: 22 – 36 months

Name ....

Date						
Age in months						

Use a different coloured pen for each assessment so that progress can be seen.

Tick 'Yes' if the child consistently demonstrates this across a range of activities, indoors and outside.

Tick 'Sometimes' if the child sometimes demonstrates this, or only demonstrates it in one or two ways or situations, or usually needs adult support.

Tick 'Rarely' if the child rarely or never demonstrates this.

	Yes	Some difficulty	Severe difficulty
Numbers			
Counts a given number of objects into the practitioner's hand one at a time.			
Sometimes recites numbers in their play.			
Shows an interest in **mathematical graphics** by choosing to mark make their own 'numbers' during play.			
Able to make some comparison of **quantity**.			
Sometimes uses language relating to **quantity** appropriately in their play.			
Understands that if someone adds another carriage to the train there are now more.			
Understands that if someone takes a carriage from the train there are now less.			
Shape, space and measures			
Points to simple shapes and patterns when prompted.			
Sometimes sorts objects according to properties of their own choosing.			
Beginning to use the language of size in their self-initiated play.			
Sometimes uses language relating to their immediate past or future.			
Anticipates some time-based events.			

Time to Discover Maths © Trudi Fitzhenry and Karen Murphy, published by Featherstone 2016

TIME TO DISCOVER MATH

Numbers - part 1

Early Years Outcomes

Uses some number names and number language spontaneously.

Uses some number names accurately in play.

Recites numbers in order to 10.

Knows that numbers identify how many objects are in a set.

Beginning to represent numbers using fingers, marks on paper or pictures.

Sometimes matches numeral and quantity correctly.

Shows curiosity about numbers by offering comments or asking questions.

Links to the Characteristics of Effective Learning

PLAYING AND EXPLORING

Finding out and exploring

★ showing curiosity about objects, events and people

★ using senses to explore the world around them

★ engaging in open-ended activity

Being willing to 'have a go'

★ initiating activities

★ seeking challenge

*e.g. the children are given cardboard strips with a numeral on to help them explore signs of autumn. Their challenge is to find the same **quantity** of objects as the **numeral** on their card. As they choose their objects they talk about how many more they need to find. Provide additional cardboard strips for children to use in their independent play.*

CREATING AND THINKING CRITICALLY

Having their own ideas

★ finding ways to solve problems

★ finding new ways to do things

Making links

★ making links and noticing patterns in their experience

★ developing ideas of grouping, sequences, cause and effect

e.g. Georgia is playing with the farm set and is putting the animals to bed. She places one animal in each stall and realises she has more animals than spaces. She goes to the creative area and selects some materials to make more beds for her animals. She then decides to number each bed, making marks to represent the numerals.

ACTIVE LEARNING

Being involved and concentrating

★ maintaining focus on their activity for a period of time

★ showing high levels of energy, fascination

Keeping on trying

★ persisting with activity when challenges occur

e.g. the children are participating in a Lego tower challenge – they take it in turns to throw a dice and collect that number of Lego pieces to add to their tower. After each turn they check to see who has the tallest tower. Chris wants to know how many blocks there are altogether after each turn and so he tries to count them. The practitioner supports him by pointing to each block as he says the number names in order.

Observation
What you may notice...

Assessment
What it may signify...

Does the child use maths related language including number names as part of their daily chatter and play?	The child has experienced maths language being used in context (e.g. when shopping or baking) and is exploring this through their play.
Does the child use the correct number names for a purpose when at play?	The child has begun to **assimilate** the number names and link them to their current play e.g. they know they will need two more cups today as there are three children and only one cup.
Can the child say the numbers from one to ten in the correct order?	The child has memorised the number names and can recite them accurately. They have learned them by rote.
Does the child ask questions about groups of objects that relate to how many there are? Can they talk about numbers in relation to the set they see?	The child is beginning to **internalise** the relationship between the number of objects they can see and the numeral that represents them.
Does the child hold up their fingers to represent a number or draw lines or marks?	The child can use their fingers, objects or **mathematical graphics** to represent a number that has meaning for them e.g. they make marks on a card to give to their friend now that they are four years old.
With support can the child match a set of objects to the correct numeral?	The child is beginning to represent items they have counted with a numeral. This is the start of early calculation.
Does the child notice **numerals** or quantities in the environment and ask questions or talk about about what they see?	The child is showing an interest in numbers and is keen to explore the everyday maths around them.

Planning
What you can do...

This links to the numbers section of the Maths Progress Checklist on p63.

Provide opportunities for maths related play to encourage the spontaneous use of maths language in the setting. For example, leave numbered empty egg cartons for children to sort conkers into or have sets of matching objects in the mud kitchen.

Draw children's attention to numbers in the environment and provide opportunities to say number names when playing. For example, provide laminated number challenges that show a picture of an object to collect and the corresponding quantity.

Sing and recite number rhymes to support children in learning number names in sequence e.g. 'One, two, three, four, five once I caught a fish alive', 'Let's count to ten' (songs and rhymes, p91).

At snack time label the plates with the **quantities** of snacks available for each group and talk to the children about what the numeral represents e.g. 'There are four pieces of apple today. Let's see if that is enough for our snack. How many people want apple? Do we have enough?'

Provide chalk and other mark-making materials so that children can choose to represent the maths in their play using symbols and mathematical graphics. For example, when keeping score in a bean bag game, model how to chalk a simple tally so the children can build on this concept. Recognise and value their efforts regardless of accuracy.

Allow time for the children to count the equipment needed for your group activity, making the marks in their own way using a clipboard and paper or whiteboard and pen. Count their marks with them and show them the corresponding numeral if they are unsure of what this looks like.

Put foam numbers 1 to 5 in the water tray and add shallow dishes and mixed plastic fruit. Can the children pick a number and fill their dish with that many pieces of fruit? Support their exploration by modelling how this can be done and by asking questions that will scaffold their thinking. e.g. 'How many bananas do you have in your dish? Let's count them - there are 4. Which number do you think is the number 4?' Leave the activity for the children to explore and note the mathematical language they use.

By 48m many children sort objects and can count and compare collections.

Additional adult-led activities

These are additional activities or guidance to further support this stage of development.

Finger fun

Play games with finger puppets to encourage the dexterity needed to be able to count using fingers. Have a different character on each finger and say 'Ollie owl is hiding away', showing the child how to isolate and bend that finger inwards. Practice with each finger in turn, then try two or three together. Add numbered stickers once children begin to recognise the numerals.

Number lines

Have number lines available both indoors and out for children to look at, play with and hop along! Laminate different shapes, sizes and colours to add interest. Leave materials ready for the children to make their own numbers to peg on a number line.

Hoop game

Support children's early recognition of the number of objects in a set through aiming beanbags into hoops on the floor. Put a large number card in each hoop and see if the child can throw the correct number in. Help them to recognise the number and offer lots of praise when they match this with beanbags!

Home-time activities

Key communication idea

Find out about number songs and rhymes shared at home, including those in a range of languages where possible, and teach these in your setting. Send home copies of new rhymes and songs learned on laminated card.

Counting steps

Place numbers in order up the stairs at home or along the hallway and recite them with your child as you climb the stairs or walk into your home. Pointing to each number in turn will support their developing number recognition.

Ten green bottles

Collect ten small plastic juice bottles (green if possible). Using an indelible marker, number the bottles from 1–10. Sing the song and enjoy knocking the bottles down one by one.

Number challenge

When out and about with your child, challenge them to spot a chosen number in the environment and count how many times they see it. For example, looking out for the number 3 on doors, billboards or car registrations. The winner earns a warm glow inside!

Glossary of terms

Set: a group or collection of objects or numbers that have something in common.

Numeral: a word or symbol used to represent a number.

Quantity: how many things there are or how much there is.

Assimilate: to take in and understand.

Internalise: absorb learning at a deeper level.

Rote learning: memorising facts through repetition.

Mathematical graphics: the marks and representations used by children to express their mathematical thoughts. The child chooses how to represent their ideas in a way that is meaningful to them.

Calculation: using maths to solve a problem and work out the answer.

Scaffold: support given to help move a child to the next level of learning.

Numbers - Part 2

Early Years Outcomes

Compares two groups of objects, saying when they have the same number.

Shows an interest in number problems.

Separates a group of three or four objects in different ways, beginning to recognise that the total is still the same.

Shows an interest in numerals in the environment.

Shows an interest in representing numbers.

Realises not only objects, but anything can be counted, including steps, claps or jumps.

Links to the Characteristics of Effective Learning

PLAYING AND EXPLORING

Finding out and exploring

★ showing curiosity about objects, events and people

★ using senses to explore the world around them

★ engaging in open-ended activity

★ showing particular interests

Being willing to 'have a go'

★ initiating activities

e.g. when the child is taking their shoes off after playing outside, they point to where the size is printed on the shoe and say 'I'm a number seven!' They turn to their friend and ask 'What number are you?'

ACTIVE LEARNING

Being involved and concentrating

★ maintaining focus on their activity for a period of time

★ showing high levels of energy, fascination

★ not easily distracted

★ paying attention to details

Keeping on trying

★ persisting with activity when challenges occur

CREATING AND THINKING CRITICALLY

Having their own ideas

★ thinking of ideas

★ finding ways to solve problems

★ finding new ways to do things

Making links

★ developing ideas of grouping, sequences, cause and effect

Choosing ways to do things

★ planning, making decisions about how to approach a task, solve a problem and reach a goal

★ checking how well their activities are going

★ reviewing how well the approach worked

e.g. Eve and Pooja are helping to harvest strawberries. They want the children to taste them and are anxious that everyone has a fair share. With support they decide to count the strawberries in groups of eight, as that matches the number of seats around the snack table. They label each bowl by copying the number 8. The last bowl only has three strawberries. They decide to save these for the adults in the room and label this bowl with a number 3. The girls are pleased when none of the children eat the spare strawberries.

30 – 50 months

Observation What you may notice...	Assessment What it may signify...
Does the child compare and comment on small groups of objects, noticing when their **quantities** match?	The child's ability to visually perceive and compare small quantities is developing in line with their ability to **subitise**.
Does the child become engaged in simple problem-solving activities and discussions when numbers are involved?	The child is showing a growing curiosity about numbers and number problems and is keen to make sense of mathematical situations.
Can the child share three or four objects between themselves and a friend so that they have more, then their friend has more, then they have the same? Can they recognise that they still have the same **total** amount that they started with?	The child's sense of **cardinality** is developing. They are beginning to understand that the last number they counted represents the total number of objects in the **set**.
Does the child pay attention to **digits** in the setting and in the world around them? Do they ask you to identify different numbers for them or can they spot familiar digits, such as their age?	The child is beginning to make explicit links between knowing number words (through rote counting, number rhymes, **one-to-one correspondence**) and seeing the number symbols in their everyday environments.
Does the child use objects or **mathematical graphics** to represent the numbers they are interested in?	The child is starting to link the marks they make or a group of objects to their ideas about number and **quantity**.
Does the child sometimes count activities or objects of their choice?	The child's interest in counting and understanding of number sequence is developing.

Planning
What you can do...

This links to the numbers section of the Maths Progress Checklist on p63.

Provide a range of large, chunky beads and cotton reels for threading. Challenge the children to match your bead string by threading on the same number. Can they say how many beads they will need? Can they match the correct amount? Can they see how many beads there are just by looking and not counting them? Encourage **one-to-one correspondence** when counting for accuracy and initially work with numbers below 5.

Share an Incy Wincy spider puppet with the children and ask them to help you work out how many wellington boots the spider will need for splashing in puddles down the spout. Prepare fewer wellington stickers than legs and allow the children to explore the spider and count the legs and boots, with your support as needed. Develop the discussion by supporting with questions such as 'How many wellington boots are there? Do we have enough? How many more will we need?'

Provide a range of opportunities for children to count small groups of objects and share them out. Encourage them to move and count each object before telling you how many there are altogether. For example, there are four aprons near the outdoor easel. Three children are painting and one apron is hanging on the peg. Can the child count the aprons and recognise there are still four altogether?

Tie some laminated, numbered luggage tags securely to a range of objects outside such as the rungs of the climbing frame or along the fence. Challenge the children to find them all and help them to recognise unfamiliar **digits**.

Take the time to listen to the children when they talk about the meaning behind the marks they make or the objects they have collected. Work alongside the child and **commentate** on what you can see. For example 'That looks like a number six' depending on the child's response, explore further number names in relation to their creation.

Play an active outdoor game involving instructions linked to counting activities. For example 'Hop, skip and jump' (see activities, songs and rhymes p91).

Additional adult-led activities

These are additional activities or guidance to further support this stage of development.

Spot the dots!

To encourage the child's ability to **subitise** introduce play with a dice that contains up to three dots. Take it in turns to roll the dice. The child who spots how many dots first is the winner! Develop this to include a fun physical challenge, so the child who does the same number of claps as dots wins etc. Gradually introduce more dots to the dice once the child can confidently recognise up to three dots.

Find a friend

For activities where children need to work in pairs, lay out some matching number and picture cards in pairs, face down. Each child chooses a card and has to find the child with the matching pictures or **digits**, who then becomes their partner. For larger groups, increase the number of matching cards.

Home-time activities

Key communication idea

Counting everyday objects together in context allows children to explore both the **stable** order of number and number **cardinality**. Counting fingers as we put them into our gloves, feet as we pop our shoes on, and grapes that we put into a bowl all offer children the chance to explore reciting numbers in order and to recognise how many there are in **total**.

Birthday numbers

Encourage your child to make birthday cards for their friends and family, showing the age. Talk about what the **digit** represents and if they show an interest, suggest they draw the corresponding number of candles, balloons or a favourite object.

Scores on the doors

When out walking with your child, draw their attention to the numbers that can be seen all around them such as on doorways, shop signs etc.

Glossary of terms

Total: the whole number or amount.

Numeral: a word or symbol used to represent a **digit**.

Digit: any one of the Arabic **numerals** 1 to 9 and the symbol 0.

Commentating: speaking out loud about what you notice the child doing while you play alongside them. This provides them with new vocabulary and models correct speech.

Subitise: the ability to recognise the number of objects in a set without counting.

Cardinality: the number of elements or objects in a group or **set**.

Set: a group or collection of objects or numbers that have something in common.

Stable order: knowing that numbers are always said in the same order.

One-to-one correspondence: being able to point to an individual object while counting and saying the correct numeral (touch counting).

Quantity: how many things there are or how much there is.

Shape, space and measure

Early Years Outcomes

Shows an interest in shape and space by playing with shapes or making arrangements with objects.

Shows awareness of similarities of shapes in the environment.

Uses positional language.

Shows interest in shape by sustained construction activity or by talking about shapes or arrangements.

Shows interest in shapes in the environment.

Uses shapes appropriately for tasks.

Beginning to talk about the shapes of everyday objects, e.g. 'round' and 'tall'.

Children begin to associate names of 2d and 3d shapes with the same size and orientation.

Links to the Characteristics of Effective Learning

PLAYING AND EXPLORING

Finding out and exploring

★ engaging in open-ended activity

★ showing curiosity about objects, events and people

Being willing to 'have a go'

★ initiating activities

★ seeking challenge

★ showing a 'can do' attitude

e.g. *Rudi is playing in the kitchen area. He asks his friends what they want for tea. Beverley says she would like fish fingers. Rudi looks in the food box for fish fingers without success. He goes to the maths area and sees a box of 3D shapes. He takes the box to the kitchen and asks Beverley to help him find some fish fingers. They sort through the box and choose some cuboids, putting them in the oven to cook.*

ACTIVE LEARNING

Being involved and concentrating

★ maintaining focus on their activity for a period of time

★ showing high levels of energy, fascination

★ not easily distracted

★ paying attention to details

Keeping on trying

★ persisting with activity when challenges occur

★ showing a belief that more effort or a different approach will pay off

★ bouncing back after difficulties

Enjoying achieving what they set out to do

★ showing satisfaction in meeting their own goals

★ being proud of how they accomplished something – not just the end result

★ enjoying meeting challenges for their own sake rather than external rewards or praise

e.g. *a group of children are trying to fit some differently shaped wooden blocks back into the box they came from. They start to place some of the blocks in the bottom but they don't fit. Annie notices that there are some lines drawn in the bottom of the box. Max looks carefully at the shape he is holding and matches it to one of the spaces created by the lines. It fits. He tells his friends they need to match the blocks to the lines so that they will fit in. The children look at their blocks and help each other to place them in the box. When they have fit them all back in, they tell the practitioner that they have tidied them all away by themselves.*

CREATING AND THINKING CRITICALLY

Having their own ideas

★ thinking of ideas

★ finding ways to solve problems

★ finding new ways to do things

Making links

★ making predictions

★ testing their ideas

Choosing ways to do things

★ planning, making decisions about how to approach a task, solve a problem and reach a goal

★ checking how well their activities are going

★ changing strategy as needed

★ reviewing how well the approach worked

e.g. Sydney is building a stable for the play horses on the farm. She chooses stackable blocks of the same size and shape and carefully pushes them onto the base. She leaves a space for the door and tries to trot her horse through this. Sydney can't fit the horse through the gap she has left. She removes some of the blocks and tries again. This time the horse fits through the door into the stable. When the practitioner asks Sydney to share how she managed to make her stable, Sydney can talk about the horse being too big for the door and how she changed her model.

Many children can now recognise and label measurable attributes of objects such as length. For example, "Is this long enough?"

Observation
What you may notice…

Assessment
What it may signify…

Observation — What you may notice…	Assessment — What it may signify…
Does the child choose to play with solidly shaped blocks, construction materials or other moveable objects to create their own representations?	The child is keen to explore different shapes and the space around and between them within a purposeful play environment.
Does the child notice and talk about similar shapes that they come across in a range of environments?	The child is making links between the shapes they have already seen and new objects that share similar properties.
Does the child talk about where objects of interest are placed either through their developing talk for play (I'm putting teddy in bed) or by linking them to a request or instruction (Can I have the brick that is on top of that shelf?).	The child's awareness of and use of **positional language** is developing in line with their practical experience of where objects are placed.
Does the child maintain concentration and interest when creating different constructions? Can they talk about what they are creating and the shapes or patterns they see?	The child's concentration span is developing in line with their fascination with the shapes, models and **patterns** they can create. They are beginning to explore the language of shape as they play.
Does the child observe shapes they know and ask questions about those that are new to them?	The child is curious about different shapes around them and keen to find out more. They are using their **visual discrimination** to identify different shapes.
Does the child find the shapes they need to complete their models, **patterns** or other creations?	The child is **assimilating** their knowledge and recognition of different shapes and their physical properties. They can use and apply this understanding in a practical manner when playing and exploring.
Is the child beginning to chat about the properties of different shapes in the environment using some mathematical terms?	The child is able to describe shapes using familiar vocabulary they have experienced in context.

Planning
What you can do...

This links to the numbers section of the Maths Progress Checklist on p63.

Have a range of solid shapes and interesting objects available in a range of provision areas for children to explore. For example, natural wooden logs in the outdoor area can be moved to create new play spaces. Mini blocks in the small world area can be placed to create enclosures or buildings with which figures can interact.

Spend time talking about the properties of different shapes and how these can be seen in everyday objects. When looking at objects that would be useful for a rolling game, draw attention to the curved faces that allow the smooth rolling action to occur. When stacking blocks to create a tower, ask the children what helps the blocks to stay in place. Explore their flat faces and compare with the bricks visible on walls outside.

Set up a seaside theme in the sand tray and challenge the children to place different objects in places guided by your use of **positional language**. For example, tell them that there are a number of shells buried under the sand for them to find. Ask them to place the crab next to the starfish and to build a sandcastle in between the tubs of water. Can they place a flag on top of their sandcastle? As you model this vocabulary the children can then begin to use it in response to questions asked about where they have placed a range of sea shells and creatures or give each other clues that are linked to a hidden object.

Have a number of construction kits and **moveable objects** available for the children to use to create their own **patterns** and representations. **Commentating** as they explore these resources will introduce the children to key vocabulary. Asking **open ended** questions such as 'Can you tell me about the pattern you have made?' or 'How can you find out which shapes you have used in your model?' will encourage the child to extend their thinking.

Have a tray of different shaped objects such as threading beads, counters, buttons, cubes, building blocks and shaped sequins. Place pictures of common **2D shapes** in the bottom of some dishes and encourage the children to sort the objects into the tray that is most like the object. Using plastic tweezers to pick up and sort the objects can also develop **fine motor** control at the same time.

Provide activities that allow children to explore how different shapes can fit together to create something new. For example, **2D shapes** made from Cellophane can be moved around a light box to make an image of a rocket or garden. Ask the child which shape they chose for the different parts or wonder with them about which shape might be good for a launch pad or for a tree.

Make sure that the language of maths is used and modelled in each area of learning so that children can link it to concrete experiences and therefore learn to understand its meaning in context. For example, when tidying away the soft play area can the children follow instructions that include shape vocabulary such as 'Look for the tall shape that can roll, can you see two round circles?'

Additional adult-led activities

These are additional activities or guidance to further support this stage of development.

Build a town

Using a range of junk materials that represent different **3D shapes** work with the children to plan and create a representation of a street or area that they know well. Can they decide which shaped box to use for different shops and buildings? How will they create roofs and chimneys? Will there be cars and other vehicles on the road? What can be used for the wheels? Allow the children to decide how to fit the different buildings together and encourage lots of language about flat or curved faces, edges etc.

Twinkle, twinkle little shape

See 'Activities, songs and rhymes' on p91 for this simple song introducing three **2D shapes**. Have a feely bag handy and reveal each shape as you sing the song. The second verse involves actions and introduces two further **2D shapes** and the sphere.

Home-time activities

Key communication idea

Share the shapes you have introduced and the linked vocabulary with parents and ask them to search for examples of everyday objects that are the same shape or have the same properties. These can be photographed, drawn or talked about in your setting to make the links between shapes and their use in the world clear.

Remote control

Use remote controlled toys or pretend your child is a robot and explore **positional language** together. Set up some simple obstacles to negotiate and give clear instructions such as move forwards, go round the teddy, travel over the book and stop next to the cushion. See if your child can be in charge of giving the commands, too!

Glossary of terms

Positional language: words that describe where an object is in relation to other objects.

Secure attachments: children who have experienced a warm and loving response at times of fear or distress are able to form secure attachments.

Pattern: a repeated sequence or design.

Concentration span: the length of time a person, or group, is able to concentrate on something or remain interested.

Moveable objects: a range of small objects that are easy to move and manipulate.

Commentating: speaking out loud about what you notice the child doing while you play alongside them. This provides them with new vocabulary and models correct speech.

Open ended/possibility questions: questions that can't be answered with one or two words. They generally require more thoughtful responses. Open ended questions usually begin with who, why, what, how or I wonder.

2-D shape: also known as 2-dimensional. A shape that only has two dimensions (such as width and height) and no thickness.

Fine motor: movements that require a high degree of control and precision. These may include drawing, writing, cutting with scissors, using cutlery.

Visual discrimination: distinguishing similarities and differences between shapes and objects.

Assimilate: to take in and understand.

3-D shape: also known as 3-dimensional. An object that has height, width and depth, like any object in the real world.

Mathematical graphics: the marks and representations used by children to express their mathematical thoughts. The child chooses how to represent their ideas in a way that is meaningful to them.

Progress Checklist: 30 – 50 months

Name ....

Date						
Age in months						

Use a different coloured pen for each assessment so that progress can be seen.

Tick 'Yes' if the child consistently demonstrates this across a range of activities, indoors and outside.

Tick 'Sometimes' if the child sometimes demonstrates this, or only demonstrates it in one or two ways or situations, or usually needs adult support.

Tick 'Rarely' if the child rarely or never demonstrates this.

	Yes	Some difficulty	Severe difficulty
Numbers			
Uses some number names and number language spontaneously.			
Uses some number names accurately in play.			
Able to recite numbers in order to 10.			
Understands that numbers identify how many objects are in a set.			
Starting to represent numbers using fingers or **mathematical graphics**.			
Sometimes matches **numeral** and **quantity** correctly.			
Talks, or asks questions about numbers.			
Compares and comments on small groups of objects, noticing when their **quantities** match.			
Becomes engaged in simple problem-solving activities and discussions when numbers are involved.			
Shares three or four objects between themselves and a friend so that they have more, then their friend has more, then they have the same. Recognises that they still have the same total amount that they started with.			
Pays attention to **digits** in the setting and in the world around them.			
Uses objects or **mathematical graphics** to represent the numbers they are interested in.			
Sometimes counts activities or objects of their choice.			
Shape, space and measures			
Chooses to play with solidly shaped blocks, construction materials or other **moveable objects** to create their own representations.			
Notices and talks about similar shapes that they come across in a range of environments.			
Talks about where objects of interest are placed either through their developing talk or play or linked to a request or instruction.			
Maintains concentration and interest when creating different constructions. Talks about what they are creating and the shapes or **patterns** they see.			
Observes shapes they know and asks questions about those that are new to them.			
Finds the shapes they need to complete their models, **patterns** or other creations.			
Beginning to chat about the properties of different shapes in the environment using some mathematical terms.			

Time to Discover Maths © Trudi Fitzhenry and Karen Murphy, published by Featherstone 2016

Numbers - part 1

arly Years Outcomes

Recognise some numerals of personal significance.

Recognise numerals 1 to 5.

Counts up to three or four objects by saying one number name for each item.

Counts actions or objects which cannot be moved.

Counts objects to 10, and beginning to count beyond 10.

Counts out up to six objects from a larger group.

Selects the correct numeral to represent 1 to 5, then 1 to 10 objects.

Counts an irregular arrangement of up to ten objects.

Links to the Characteristics of Effective Learning

CREATING AND THINKING CRITICALLY

Having their own ideas

* ★ thinking of ideas

* ★ finding ways to solve problems

* ★ finding new ways to do things

Making links

* ★ making links and noticing patterns in their experience

* ★ making predictions

* ★ testing their ideas

* ★ developing ideas of grouping, sequences, cause and effect

Choosing ways to do things

* ★ planning, making decisions about how to approach a task, solve a problem and reach a goal

* ★ checking how well their activities are going

* ★ changing strategy as needed

* ★ reviewing how well the approach worked

e.g. Neil chooses to take on the daily challenge during free-flow. The task is to find out which are the most popular activities. Instead of asking the other children he decides to watch activities and record how many children are playing with each of them. He starts at the construction area. With a clipboard and pencil he draws a picture to represent the number of children. He finds he cannot draw quickly enough so seeks adult help. He is supported with a simple **tally***. He visits several activities throughout the session. After each one he checks his* **tally** *and counting with an adult who* **scribes** *the name of the activity and the correct* **digit***.*

PLAYING AND EXPLORING

Finding out and exploring

* ★ showing curiosity about objects, events and people

* ★ using senses to explore the world around them

* ★ showing particular interests

Playing with what they know

* ★ acting out experiences with other people

Being willing to 'have a go'

* ★ initiating activities

* ★ seeking challenge

e.g. Chloe and Zane are outside digging. Chloe finds a worm. She tells Zane that she and her brother have worm hunts at home. She challenges Zane. They spend the morning each collecting worms in a bucket, keeping score as they go. After a final count a draw is declared and the worms are put back in the soil.

ACTIVE LEARNING

Being involved and concentrating

★ maintaining focus on their activity for a period of time

★ showing high levels of energy, fascination

★ not easily distracted

★ paying attention to details

Keeping on trying

★ persisting with activity when challenges occur

★ showing a belief that more effort or a different approach will pay off

★ bouncing back after difficulties

Enjoying achieving what they set out to do

★ showing satisfaction in meeting their own goals

★ being proud of how they accomplished something – not just the end result

★ enjoying meeting challenges for their own sake rather than external rewards or praise

e.g. X and Y have a selection of small plastic numbered bottles and some boxes with corresponding numbers on the front. They recycle the bottles by putting them in the matching box.

Observation What you may notice…		Assessment What it may signify…
Does the child talk about and point out numbers that are important to them, for example their age?	▷	The child is developing their **number sense** and is becoming more familiar with numbers that hold personal meaning for them. They are developing their **visual discrimination** skills in order to identify the different **numerals**.
Can the child find the **digits** 1 to 5 in response to the corresponding number name?	▷	The child is beginning to link the abstract symbol (the printed **digit**) with the number name. Their understanding of the relationship between **rote-learned** numbers and their corresponding symbols is growing.
Can the child count up to four objects by pointing to them or moving them as they say the numbers in sequence?	▷	The child has a secure sense of **stable order** when counting up to four objects.
Can the child count a number of fixed objects using **one-to-one correspondence**?	▷	The child is showing an ability to touch and count static objects e.g. coat pegs on a wall using the correct number sequence.
Can the child say the number names in sequence to ten and beyond? Can they accurately count ten or more objects?	▷	The child has a secure understanding of **stable order** to ten and beyond and can recite the number names in sequence. They know that each object is counted only once and is linked to one number name in the sequence.

Planning
What you can do...

This links to the numbers section of the Maths Progress Checklist on p88.

Develop a number rich environment both inside and outdoors. Ensure children have access to numbers in the sand tray, the water tray, on number lines and in the construction area. Use permanent pen to write numbers on pebbles or bottle tops for sorting or burying. Number pots and pans and their corresponding hooks in the mud kitchen and role-play areas. Encourage children to notice and say the number names as part of their play.

Provide a range of numbered items for the children to access as part of your ongoing role-play provision. These could include calculators, push button telephones and telephones with dials. Leave short 'telephone numbers' on card for the children to notice and model how to dial/press these in sequence, saying the number names. Increase the length and digit span of the telephone numbers as children's confidence increases.

When teaching children how to count accurately, provide them with a range of interesting objects to count including buttons, toys, fir cones, pennies, paper clips or bottle tops. Model how to move and count one object at a time and place each object into an empty egg box or paint palette, to give the child a sense of the **quantity** increasing as the number names are spoken.

To further develop confidence in **one-to-one correspondence**, set matching tasks for the children to complete. For example, can they give each child a paper towel before they wash their hands? Are their enough towels? Can they make sure that every whiteboard has a pen? Are there enough blue pencils for everyone in the group?

By the age of five, most children can organise objects or pictures into simple charts or graphs and count how many there are in each group.

Singing counting songs and rhymes while using objects to model the counting can really help to embed children's understanding of number order. Young children are naturally curious about larger numbers, so include songs that go beyond 20 to increase their awareness of these. Look at 'The Big Numbers' song on YouTube as a good example.

By age four and a half most children can add quantities by counting all of the objects.

Observation
What you may notice...

Assessment
What it may signify...

Can the child retrieve a given number of objects from a larger group when asked to find an amount up to six?

The child is demonstrating both accuracy in counting and an awareness of **cardinality**. They are showing an ability to reach a given number without counting past it. Their counting skills are becoming secure.

Can the child match a number card to the corresponding group of objects up to ten?

The child's understanding of **numerals** as symbols and matching **quantities** is developing. They have begun to grasp **cardinality** in relation to the total number of objects in each set.

Can the child accurately count objects that are not in sequence through **one-to-one correspondence**?

The child can use discrete counting and accurate **one-to-one correspondence** to find the **total** number of objects. They can integrate saying the correct number name with pointing at each object.

Planning
What you can do...

This links to the numbers section of the Maths Progress Checklist on p88.

If the child struggles with the number you have requested, try lowering this until you reach a number that is within their conceptual range. Playing shopping with a mini basket and shopping list showing both the **digit** and a picture of the **quantity** of items you need can encourage the child to count out and match the desired amount.

Hide different quantities of objects in lidded boxes and prepare some cards that show the numbers to ten. Can the children explore the sounds each box makes when it is shaken and decide which box they think has the smallest or largest quantity of objects in it? Can they place a number card next to the box they think holds that amount? Finally, can they count and check that the quantities and numbers match?

How many opportunities for counting a range of pictures, images or objects are there in your learning environment? Consider placing counting challenges in different areas for the children to find and complete. For example, how many butterflies are on the fence outside? How many car paintings are on the display? How many children are in our group today? How many tyres are on the grass? How many taps in the cloakroom? How many numbers can you see on the clock face? This can be set as a treasure hunt type challenge or be part of the everyday maths conversations that take place in your setting.

Additional adult-led activities

These are additional activities or guidance to further support this stage of development.

Count down

When children listen to adults counting they **assimilate** the **stable order** of numbers. Counting beyond ten and 20 models what happens when you cross a tens threshold and counting backwards prepares them for early subtraction.

Code breaker

Create a toy treasure chest with a combination lock on it that the children need to manipulate to get inside. Change the combination each day but keep it in numerical order so the children can practice these sequences. For example start with 1, 2, 3, 4 then move on to 2, 3, 4, 5 etc.

Home-time activities

Key communication idea

With parents, choose a number that children can look out for and practice identifying. They could take pictures of it, have a go at forming it themselves or cut pictures of it out of magazines or newspapers and make a poster.

Match making

When adults involve children in matching and counting everyday objects it deepens their awareness of the relationship between abstract number names and physical things. When writing invitations or cards, allow the child to match them to the envelopes and count them. This practises **one-to-one correspondence**.

Time for tea

When preparing a meal at home, involve your child in counting how many things you will need to make or prepare. Can they count out the correct number of plates for the sandwiches or make sure that everyone has a biscuit each?

Glossary of terms

Numeral: a word or symbol used to represent a **digit**.

Tally: a form of numeral used for counting. It is common to tally using straight lines. Once children start to count in fives use four vertical lines and one diagonal line to represent a group of five.

Scribe: to write down a child's words on their behalf as spoken.

Digit: any one of the Arabic **numerals** 1 to 9 and the symbol 0.

Numeral: a word or symbol used to represent a **digit**.

One-to-one correspondence: being able to point to an individual object while counting and saying the correct numeral (touch counting).

Total: the whole number or amount.

Number sense: the child's inner understanding of numbers, what they mean and their relationship to one another including within a problem.

Visual discrimination: distinguishing similarities and differences between shapes and objects.

Rote learning: memorising facts through repetition.

Stable order: knowing that numbers are always said in the same order.

Quantity: how many things there are or how much there is.

Assimilate: to take in and understand.

Cardinality: the number of elements or objects in a group or **set**.

Quantity: how many things there are or how much there is.

Discrete counting: counting things using numbers in order to find out how many there are.

Numbers - part 2

Early Years Outcomes

Estimates how many objects they can see and checks by counting them.

Uses the language of 'more' and 'fewer' to compare two **sets** of objects.

Finds the **total** number of items in two groups by counting all of them.

Says the number that is one more than a given number.

Finds one more or one less from a group of up to five objects, then ten objects.

In practical activities and discussion, beginning to use the vocabulary involved in **adding** and **subtracting**.

Records, using marks that they can interpret and explain.

Begins to identify own mathematical problems based on own interests and fascinations.

Early Learning Goal (ELG)
Children count reliably with numbers from one to 20, place them in order and say which number is one more or one less than a given number. Using quantities and objects, they add and subtract two single-digit numbers and count on or back to find an answer. They solve problems, including doubling, halving and sharing.

The ELG is a description of typical attainment at the end of the EYFS. If the child consistently demonstrates elements (though not necessarily all) of the ELG in a range of situations, and with familiar and unfamiliar adults and peers, then it is likely that the child is at the expected level. Practitioners should refer to the Statutory Framework for the EYFS, the Foundation Stage Profile handbook and exemplification materials (**www.gov.uk** or **www.foundationyears.org.uk**).

Meeting the ELG signifies that the practitioner judges the child's **summative** development to be at the expected level for the end of the EYFS.

Links to the Characteristics of Effective Learning

PLAYING AND EXPLORING

Finding out and exploring

★ showing particular interests

Playing with what they know

★ pretending objects are things from their experience

★ representing their experiences in play

★ taking on a role in their play

★ acting out experiences with other people

Being willing to 'have a go'

★ initiating activities

★ seeking challenge

★ showing a 'can do' attitude

★ taking a risk, engaging in new experiences, and learning by trial and error

*e.g. Mia is playing in the bakery. She remembers that her mum bought some doughnuts but there aren't any to sell. She goes to the playdough and tries to make some. After several attempts and a little adult support she is happy with the result. She puts them on a tray, returns to the bakery and sells them to her friends. Each one costs 1p. She is able to **calculate** the cost of up to five doughnuts and give change from ten single pennies.*

ACTIVE LEARNING

Being involved and concentrating

★ maintaining focus on their activity for a period of time

★ showing high levels of energy, fascination

★ not easily distracted

★ paying attention to details

Keeping on trying

★ persisting with activity when challenges occur

★ showing a belief that more effort or a different approach will pay off

★ bouncing back after difficulties

Enjoying achieving what they set out to do

★ showing satisfaction in meeting their own goals

★ being proud of how they accomplished something – not just the end result

★ enjoying meeting challenges for their own sake rather than external rewards or praise

e.g. Dane is playing with a number line floor puzzle. He counts out loud to himself as he puts the pieces in order. He reaches 14 and discovers the piece is missing. He looks around but cannot find it. After a few moments he finds a wooden 1 and a 4 and puts them in the space then continues with the puzzle to 20. Looking at the 14 he decides to try and make a puzzle piece. He gets paper, scissors and a crayon. He copies the wooden shapes, reversing the numbers. He seeks out a practitioner who helps him re-write the number and cut out a suitable shape to replace the wooden numbers. When it is finished he looks at it, smiles then takes a photo to show his dad at the end of the day.

CREATING AND THINKING CRITICALLY

Having their own ideas

★ thinking of ideas

★ finding ways to solve problems

★ finding new ways to do things

Making links

★ making links and noticing patterns in their experience

★ making predictions

★ testing their ideas

★ developing ideas of grouping, sequences, cause and effect

Choosing ways to do things

★ planning, making decisions about how to approach a task, solve a problem and reach a goal

e.g. *Poonam is sorting some leaves she has found. She has put them in sets based on their colour. Toby asks her if he can have some of her leaves for his picture. Poonam looks carefully at her piles of leaves and decides to give Toby some yellow ones. When Toby asks for some red leaves, Poonam tells him he has to have yellow because she has more of those.*

40 – 60+ months

Observation
What you may notice…

Assessment
What it may signify…

Observation	Assessment
Is the child willing to have a good guess as to the number of objects they can see? Can they then count them using **one-to-one correspondence** for accuracy?	The child's confidence in their own **number sense** is growing. They are prepared to take a risk through **estimating** without needing to be exactly right.
Can the child say which **set** has got the most or least amount of objects? Do they use the terms 'more' and 'fewer'?	The child can **visually discriminate** between two groups of objects. They can talk about which group has more and which has fewer.
Will the child count two groups of objects and say how many there are altogether?	The child is able to keep track of the objects they have counted and can recognise that the **total** number of objects has changed.
Does the child know the number that comes after a given number? Can they recognise that this means it is worth one more than the given number?	The child has a secure understanding of number order. They are beginning to understand that the next number in the sequence represents more.
Can the child work out what one more or one less will be by adding to or taking away from a group of objects (with no more than 10 objects)?	The child is beginning to explore the concepts of **addition** and **subtraction**.
Does the child talk about how many objects there are altogether? Do they notice who has most or least or suggest ways to **increase** or **decrease quantities** when playing or sharing resources?	The child is **assimilating** the language involved in addition and subtraction. They are developing their understanding and use of terms such as more, fewer, less than, altogether, add, take away, how many, and, difference between, **sum, total**.
Does the child show an interest in recording their maths thinking skills using available materials? Can they talk about what they have drawn or made and what it means to them?	The child is developing their personal representations of the maths they experience and using **mathematical graphics** to assign meaning to this. They are able to record their own maths thinking rather than record in response to an adult's suggestion.
Does the child look for ways to solve problems involving number, quantity and simple **calculations** as they explore their own ideas and interests?	The child is consolidating their **number sense** through exploring ways in which numbers link to the world around them and **calculations** can be used to solve practical problems of their choosing.

Planning
What you can do...

This links to the numbers section of the Maths Progress Checklist on p88.

Estimation can occur naturally throughout the day. Encourage children to have a good guess at how many pencils there are in the pot before sharing them out, how many children are having lunch, how many pictures there are on the window etc. Next help them to point and count the **total** so you can both compare how close their **estimation** was. Remember to praise their good guesses to build their confidence!

Model the use of the terms 'more' and 'fewer' so the children **assimilate** these. Ask questions such as 'Who has the most blocks? Who has the least?' and **commentate** as they play. For example 'Sara has fewer blue beads than you. Do you have more red beads?'

Using objects that can be easily manipulated will support the child's developing understanding of **addition**. When finding the **total** the child may be able to **subitise** smaller numbers and count on from there. For example they may see there are three starfish and then count on four more to reach a **total** of seven. It is important to use actual objects so the child can see how the **total** increases as you add more on.

Share puzzles and number lines that represent both the numbers and their equivalent amounts in pictures. Ask the child 'What comes next after four?' and help them to notice that there are more apples next to number four than bananas next to number three and this is because as the number gets higher or further to the right on a number line the value increases.

Play number games involving number lines where the children can physically move along the line to find one more or one less. For example, place some beanbags along floor tiles that are ordered to ten. Challenge the children in turn to stand on the number that is one more than/one less than the number where the beanbag is resting. If they are correct, they collect the beanbag. Continue using numbers up to 20 when children are secure when dealing with ten or less.

As the children gain confidence with **calculations** create puzzles for them to solve at the start of each day. Have a selection of locks with different numbers on them. Tie a luggage tag to the corresponding keys that shows a pictorial addition or subtraction for the children to solve. When they match the problem with the correct answer the lock will open.

In order to encourage the development of **mathematical graphics** ensure there is a range of mark making materials in the maths workshop area for children to use. Scribe and display the children's mathematical questions, problem solving and their own **mathematical graphics** to show these are valued.

Provide opportunities for open-ended investigations in each learning area that link to maths. Use **open-ended questions** to encourage problem solving such as 'How can we count these buttons?', 'How many ways can we make a **total** of six?', 'Can you put these in order? How did you choose to do that?', 'Can you find a way to share the magnets?'

Additional adult-led activities

These are additional activities or guidance to further support this stage of development.

Penny drop

To encourage **estimation** and counting while developing listening skills, ask the child to guess how many coins you drop into a tin by listening to the sound they make as they fall. Then, tip out the coins and count them together. Model different strategies for counting, including lining the coins up, moving them one at a time and touch counting.

Crayon sort

Use coloured bowls to sort crayons and see if the children can talk about which colour has the most or least amount. Can they share the crayons between their friends? How many does each child get? Can they find the difference between the number of green and blue crayons? Encourage them to find their own ways of using the crayons to record their results.

Home-time activities

Key communication idea

Share the mathematical language used in your setting or classroom so that parents can talk about solving problems in the same way. Having a mini maths dictionary (use the glossary on p94 as a starting point) that is shared can introduce parents to key vocabulary and build their confidence when talking to their child about counting, **estimating** and **calculating**.

Money matching

Having a selection of money for children to sort and count can provide lots of fun. Use empty plastic tubs and stick one different coin in the bottom of each one. Encourage your child to name and sort the rest of the coins to match the one in each tub. Then, explore how many there are of each kind and which tub contains the most or least. This activity is useful for developing coin recognition and counting coins as objects, not linked to their **value**.

Glossary of terms

Estimate: an informed guess at how many or how much.

Set: a group or collection of objects or numbers that have something in common.

Total: the whole number or amount.

Addition: finding the total of two or more numbe

Subtraction: taking one number away from another.

Sum: the **total** of two or more amounts.

One-to-one correspondence: being able to point to an individual object while counting and saying the correct numeral (touch counting).

Quantity: how much of something there is.

Increase: to become greater or larger in amour or size.

Decrease: to become smaller or fewer in amount or size.

Subitise: the ability to recognise the number of objects in a set without counting.

Mathematical graphics: the marks and representations used by children to express their mathematical thoughts.

Calculation: a process involving **addition**, **subtraction**, **multiplication** or **division** that requires careful thought.

Number sense: the child's inner understanding of numbers, what they mean and their relationsh to one another including within a problem.

Visual discrimination: distinguishing similariti and differences between quantities, shapes and objects.

Assimilate: to take in and understand.

Commentating: speaking out loud about what you notice the child doing while you play alongsid them. This provides them with new vocabulary and models correct speech.

Summative: an end assessment of a child's learning or development.

Value: how much an object or coin is worth.

Shape, space and measures

Early Years Outcomes

Beginning to use mathematical names for 'solid' 3-D shapes and 'flat' 2-D shapes, and mathematical terms to describe shapes.

Selects a particular named shape.

Can describe their relative position such as 'behind' or 'next to'.

Orders two or three items by length or height.

Orders two items by weight or capacity.

Uses familiar objects and common shapes to create and recreate patterns and build models.

Uses everyday language related to time.

Beginning to use everyday language related to money.

Orders and sequences familiar events.

Measures short periods of time in simple ways.

Early Learning Goal (ELG). Children use everyday language to talk about size, weight, capacity, position, distance, time and money to compare quantities and objects to solve problems. They recognise, create and describe patterns. They explore characteristics of everyday objects and shapes and use mathematical language to describe them.

Links to the Characteristics of Effective Learning

<table>
<tr><td>

PLAYING AND EXPLORING

Finding out and exploring

★ showing particular interests

Playing with what they know

★ representing their experiences in play

★ taking on a role in their play

★ acting out experiences with other people

Being willing to 'have a go'

★ initiating activities

★ seeking challenge

★ showing a 'can do' attitude

e.g. after the summer fair the children decide to recreate some of the stalls they enjoyed. With adult support they fill the paddling pool and find the 'hook a duck' and 'magnetic fish' games. They make posters to advertise their games, collect a till and some money then start charging their friends for a go.

</td><td>

ACTIVE LEARNING

Being involved and concentrating

★ maintaining focus on their activity for a period of time

★ showing high levels of energy, fascination

★ not easily distracted

★ paying attention to details

Keeping on trying

★ persisting with activity when challenges occur

★ showing a belief that more effort or a different approach will pay off

★ bouncing back after difficulties

Enjoying achieving what they set out to do

★ enjoying meeting challenges for their own sake rather than external rewards or praise

e.g. the children are role playing being at the car wash. They want to use the hose on the water wall to wash the vehicles. They try unsuccessfully to get the hose to work. After several attempts and lots of discussion they realise that they need the water to reach a certain level for the mechanism to work. One of the children suggests they need a bigger bucket and lots more water. Another child goes inside and returns with two large buckets. Working cooperatively they achieve their objective and the vehicles get cleaned.

</td></tr>
</table>

CREATING AND THINKING CRITICALLY

Having their own ideas

★ thinking of ideas

★ finding ways to solve problems

★ finding new ways to do things

Making links

★ making links and noticing patterns in their experience

★ making predictions

★ testing their ideas

★ developing ideas of grouping, sequences, cause and effect

Choosing ways to do things

★ planning, making decisions about how to approach a task, solve a problem and reach a goal

★ checking how well their activities are going

★ changing strategy as needed

★ reviewing how well the approach worked

e.g. *the daily maths challenge involves a basket of muddled clothes that need sorting on the washing line. The children start by making a simple pattern of, red sock, blue sock, red sock, blue sock. Pleased with the result they call a practitioner to look. As the children find this quite easy the practitioner challenges them to include all of the items in their pattern. They take down the first pattern, then keep trying new ideas until finally they have included all the items in their new design.*

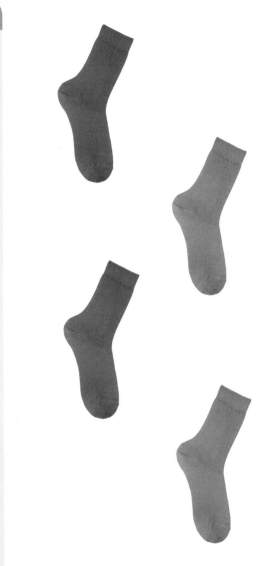

Observation **What you may notice...**		Assessment **What it may signify...**
Does the child use some shape names (e.g. triangle, circle, cube) when talking about the shapes they see? Can they describe shapes using words such as straight, curved, side?	▶	The child is beginning to link familiar shapes to their names. They are starting to recognise that shapes have certain properties that can be described e.g. a square has four sides.
Can the child find a named shape from a selection shown?	▶	The child can **visually discriminate** between different shapes and has **internalised** shape names.
Can the child describe where they are in relation to other children or places in the setting?	▶	The child is developing their **spatial awareness** and can describe this using **positional language**.
Can the child compare how long or how tall objects are and order them from the shortest to the longest or tallest?	▶	The child is beginning to **visually discriminate** between different lengths and heights and is developing an understanding of how to compare these. They are using their **non-measuring reasoning** and are developing the concept of **transitivity**.
Can the child compare how heavy or light objects are? Can they compare how full or empty containers are?	▶	The child is developing their understanding of **mass** and **capacity** through practical activities involving weighing and measuring.

Planning
What you can do...

This links to the space, shape and measures section of the Maths Progress Checklist on p89.

Talk about shapes in the environment and use mathematical vocabulary when describing the shapes you can see. For example, when sorting equipment for games outside, ask the children to find all of the objects that have a curved face to put in the basket. Do they link this to the balls they need to collect? Have another basket for the objects that have four straight sides and four corners – can the children place the beanbags in here?

Having accessible pictures of shapes in both outdoor and indoor learning environments will allow children to recognise their features. Provide shape templates for children to draw around, squeezy shapes in the water, shape lotto games for matching and recognition. Playing games such as 'Shape reveal' (see activities, songs and rhymes p91) can help children to identify shape features and link these to the correct shape name.

Playing games such as 'Hide and seek' can be a fun way to help children to develop both **spatial awareness** and **positional language**. Hide a toy somewhere in the setting (this can be played outdoors or in) and encourage the children to ask questions in order to find it. Model questions for them at first, such as, 'Is teddy hiding under the blanket?', 'Have you checked inside the book box?', 'Is he hiding next to the train track?' As the children move to each area, notice how they respond to the positional language used. This game can be developed so that the children lead and give each other instructions on how to find the hidden toy.

Talk about the comparative sizes of different objects so the child hears the use of mathematical language in context. Address potential misconceptions relating to size by showing children how to compare objects fairly e.g. by lining up different objects along the same point before judging which is longer or shorter. Lots of measuring activities comparing a range of ribbons, straws, toys and pencils of different lengths and heights will encourage the development of **non-measuring** reasoning and **transitivity**.

Exploration of **capacity** can take place wherever there are empty containers of varying shapes and sizes and a range of resources that can be used to fill them. Provide tubs, bowls, youghurt pots and tubes in the maths area to be filled with counters, buttons, conkers or cubes. Have empty, clean household bottles and jugs in the water tray and explore the concepts of full and overflowing. Pots, pans and dishes in the mud kitchen can be emptied or filled with soil and water. Buckets, moulds and beakers can be used in the sand tray. Link **capacity** with **mass** through posing questions about how much different containers weigh when they are full or empty and each of the stages inbetween, thinking carefully about different sizes and shapes and how they may look heavier or to have greater **capacity** but we need to check as sometimes the shorter, wider containers hold and therefore weigh more.

By four and a half, most children can use non-standard units of measure to compare how empty or full different containers are.

Observation
What you may notice...

Assessment
What it may signify...

Does the child create their own repeating patterns or models using a range of objects or shapes?

The child is developing their problem-solving skills and ability to make links between the **concrete** objects they manipulate and **abstract** reasoning about patterns and connections.

Does the child talk about different times of the day or year, or comment on the passing of time in relation to how long things take or when important events will happen?

The child is beginning to understand time as something that can be measured.

Does the child talk about buying or selling things in their play and use words relating to how much things cost or **currency** they are using?

The child is aware of money as a means of buying things. They are starting to explore the language they hear adults use in relation to money through their play.

Does the child show an awareness of familiar events during the day? Can they tell you what comes next in a familiar timetabled sequence?

The child recognises that events can be repeated and that some events are linked to a certain day or time of day.

Does the child show an interest in finding out how long an activity or a period of time will take? Can they suggest ways of measuring how the time passes?

The child is becoming aware of the length of time different activities take and is showing an interest in how to measure this.

The ELG is a description of typical attainment at the end of the EYFS. If the child consistently demonstrates elements (though not necessarily all) of the ELG in a range of situations, and with familiar and unfamiliar adults and peers, then it is likely that the child is at the expected level. Practitioners should refer to the Statutory Framework for the EYFS, the Foundation Stage Profile handbook and exemplification materials (www.gov.uk or www.foundationyears.org.uk).

Meeting the ELG signifies that the practitioner judges the child's **summative** development to be at the expected level for the end of the EYFS.

Planning
What you can do...

This links to the space, shape and measures section of the Maths Progress Checklist on p89.

Encourage children to look for and notice patterns in the natural world: the whorls on a snail shell, the rings in a tree trunk, the spots on a ladybird. Use snack time to talk about patterns and arrange the fruit and vegetables in a simple repeating pattern. See if the children can continue it e.g. apple, carrot, apple, carrot... Can they draw or paint a pattern they have seen or made?

Many children enjoy talking about important events in their lives through sharing news and pictures with their group. Use these occasions to draw a link between things that have already happened in the past, those that will happen in the future and the vocabulary that identifies these. For example, talking about before, after, yesterday, tomorrow, next week in context will help children to understand the meaning of these words. Similarly, if you ask a child to wait a minute use a sand timer so they can begin to notice how long a minute actually is!

Role-play areas are a great way to allow children to identify the different coins and notes that make up our **currency** while developing their understanding of buying, selling and giving change. Take time to **commentate** as you play alongside the child, asking how much things cost and exclaiming that it is too expensive, do they have anything cheaper as you only have £1 etc. Price objects in your café, shop or garden centre so children become familiar with the £ and p symbols. Model counting coins out to pay for goods so that children learn that different coins can be counted in different ways dependent on their **value**.

Make time each day to talk the children through the planned routies and activities so they begin to understand the daily sequence of events. Share pictures at the end of the week showing which activities the children have enjoyed and what they discovered each day. This will introduce them to the names of the days of the week and enable them to link these to the activities that take place.

Children quite often find measuring time useful if they are waiting for their turn with a particular toy or activity. Setting a simple timeframe linked to 'before and after' can help children to measure the time between their turn and another child's. For example, 'Can you collect all of the cones before you have a turn on the trike?' or, 'After Zara has coloured in her fish, you can have the green pencil.' As children become more aware of standard units of time, sand timers can be introduced to show the passage of time in minutes.

Additional adult-led activities

These are additional activities or guidance to further support this stage of development.

Musical shapes

Chalk 2-D shapes on the ground outside and play a musical game with the children. They dance around the shapes and when the music stops, stand in a shape that you call out. You can easily observe which shapes they recognise and which they are unsure of. Make this more challenging by describing the shape properties and ask the children to shout out the shape name when they stand in it!

Parcel puzzle

A common misconception when comparing the weight of objects is that larger means heavier and smaller means lighter. Wrap a range of different sized boxes in brown parcel paper and fill some with bags of rice, making sure the smaller items are the heaviest. Encourage the children to talk about which parcel they think will be the heaviest and why, before lifting them to sort them into groups of heavy and light. Support the children's discussion and encourage use of mathematical language as they explore different weights in this investigation.

Home-time activities

Key communication idea

Create a mini shape bag with 2-D shapes clearly labelled with their name and properties e.g. 'I am a square. I have four straight sides that are all the same length and one flat face. I have four corners.' This can be taken home to use as a discussion prompt or to encourage children to create their own shape characters.

Money, money, money

Children love to sort and play with coins and will benefit from learning how to recognise our **currency**. Talk to them about the size, shape and colour of each coin as well as its **value**. Help them to count the total number of coins and then look together at the total **value** – explaining how the number on the coin represents what it is worth.

Balanced buns!

Use a set of balances to explore weight and measures while baking some delicious buns. Place two eggs (in their shells) on one side of the balance and help your child to measure out butter, sugar and flour in turn so that their weight balances with the eggs. Discuss how heavy or light different ingredients are and how much or little is needed of each as compared to the eggs. Once this is done, mix the ingredients together with an electric whisk (or by hand, starting with creaming the butter and sugar before adding the eggs and self-raising flour) adding a splash of milk if the batter needs loosening. Spoon into bun cases while talking about the **capacity** of each case and if it is full or half full. Bake in a pre-heated oven at 180C/350F/Gas 4 for 8 to 10 minutes or until golden brown on top. Talk to your child about the passing of time and how long the cakes take to bake.

Glossary of terms

-D shape: also known as 2-dimensional. A hape that only has two dimensions (such as idth and height) and no thickness.

-D shape: also known as 3-dimensional. An oject that has height, width and depth, like any oject in the real world.

apacity: the amount something can contain.

isual discrimination: distinguishing milarities and differences between shapes and ojects.

ternalise: absorb learning at a deeper level.

patial awareness: the recognition of the stance between objects and the ability to judge here you are in relation to objects.

ositional language: words that describe here an object is in relation to other objects.

on-measuring reasoning: comparing ojects by looking at their size in relation to each her.

Transitivity: knowing that an object is longer or shorter than another through direct comparison with a third object.

Commentating: speaking out loud about what you notice the child doing while you play alongside them. This provides them with new vocabulary and models correct speech.

Mass: how much matter is in an object, which is measured in grams and kilograms.

Concrete: something real that exists in a physical form.

Abstract: something that exists as an idea or thought.

Summative: an end assessment of a child's learning or development.

Currency: a country's money system.

Value: how much something is worth.

Progress Checklist: 40 – 60+ months

Name ....

Date						
Age in months						

Use a different coloured pen for each assessment so that progress can be seen.

Tick 'Yes' if the child consistently demonstrates this across a range of activities, indoors and outside.

Tick 'Sometimes' if the child sometimes demonstrates this, or only demonstrates it in one or two ways or situations, or usually needs adult support.

Tick 'Rarely' if the child rarely or never demonstrates this.

	Yes	Some difficulty	Severe difficulty
Numbers			
Talks about and points out numbers that are important to them, for example their age.			
Finds the **digits** 1 to 5 in response to the corresponding number name.			
Counts up to four objects by pointing to them or moving them as they say the numbers in sequence.			
Counts a number of fixed objects using **one-to-one correspondence**.			
Says the number names in sequence to ten and beyond.			
Accurately counts ten or more objects.			
Retrieves a given number of objects from a larger group when asked to find an amount up to six.			
Matches a number card to the corresponding group of objects up to ten.			
Accurately counts objects that are not in sequence through **one-to-one correspondence**.			
Willing to have a good guess as to the number of objects they can see. Counts them using **one-to-one correspondence** for accuracy.			
Says which **set** has got the most or least amount of objects. Uses the terms 'more' and 'fewer'.			
Counts two groups of objects and says how many there are altogether.			
Knows the number that comes after a given number. Recognises that this means it is worth one more than the given number.			
Works out what one more or one less will be by adding to or taking away from a group of objects within ten.			
Talks about how many objects there are altogether. Notices who has most or least or suggests ways to **increase** or **decrease quantities** when playing or sharing resources.			
Shows an interest in recording their mathematical thinking using available materials. Talks about what they have drawn or made and what it means to them.			
Looks for ways to solve problems involving number, quantity and simple calculations as they explore their own ideas and follow their interests.			

	Yes	Some difficulty	Severe difficulty
ape, space and measures			
es some shape names (e.g. triangle, circle, cube) when talking about the apes they see.			
scribes shapes using words such as straight, curved, side.			
ds a named shape from a selection shown.			
scribes where they are in relation to other children or places in the setting.			
mpares how long or how tall objects are and orders them from the shortest to e longest or tallest.			
mpares how heavy or light objects are.			
mpares how full or empty containers are.			
eates their own repeating patterns or models using a range of objects or apes.			
ks about different times of the day or year, or comments on the passing of time relation to how long things take or when important events will happen.			
ks about buying or selling things in their play and uses words relating to how ch things cost or currency they are using.			
ows an awareness of familiar events during the day. Can say what comes next a familiar timetabled sequence.			
ows an interest in finding out how long an activity or a period of time will take.			
n suggest ways of measuring how the time passes.			

to Discover Maths © Trudi Fitzhenry and Karen Murphy, published by Featherstone 2016

TIME TO DISCOVER M

Activities, songs and rhymes

One, two where are your shoes?

One, two where are your shoes?
Sing/say tapping one foot then the other as you say one, two
Three, four they're on the floor
Sing/say as you point to the shoes or tap each one on the floor
Five, six put them on quick
Sing/say as you put the shoes on or support the child to put them on themselves
Seven, eight we won't be late
Sing/say and clap on eight
Hurray!
Say as you celebrate with a smile and a cheer.

One, two, three what can we see?

One, two, three What can we see? What can we see today?
Say rhyme as you look around holding your hand above your eyes as a visor
I can see a ….
Say this slowly as you move you arm to point to the object and draw the child's attention towards it
Big, black bird sitting on the wall
Repeat.
Continue, changing the last line for different objects and events, using the language of size, shape and position.

One, two, three sing with me

One, two, three, sing with me, sing with me to one, two, three
One, two, three, clap with me, clap with me to one, two, three
Clap the child's hands in time to the words
One, two, three, wave with me, wave with me to one, two, three
Wave the child's hands in time to the words
One, two, three, tap your knee, tap your knee to one, two, three
Tap the child's hand on their knee in time to the words
(add actions such as hop, jump and run for older children)

Two little pretty birds

Two little pretty birds sitting on a wall –
make a fist, pop index fingers up and wiggle them
One named Peter
Wiggle the left finger
One named Paul
Wiggle the right finger
Fly away Peter
Put your left hand behind your back
Fly away Paul
Put your right hand behind your back
Come back Peter
Bring Peter back
Come back Paul
Bring Paul back

Two little hands

Two little hands go clap, clap, clap
Two little feet go tap, tap, tap
Two little arms wave up and down
Two little legs just jiggle around
Two little eyes look left and right
then close up tight and say goodnight
goodnight!

Baa, baa black sheep

Baa, baa black sheep
Have you any wool?
Yes sir, yes sir
Three bags full!
One for the master and one for the dame
One for the little girl who lives down the lane
Thank you said the master
Thank you said the dame
Thank you said the little girl who lives down the lane.

Counting sheep

(To the tune of Ten green bottles)
One sleepy sheep is ready for his bed
One sleepy sheep lays down his sleepy head
Night, night everyone the sleepy sheep said
Night, night sleepy sheep it's time for bed!

Two sleepy sheep are ready for their bed
Two sleepy sheep lay down their sleepy heads...
(Continue this increase the number of sheep each time.)

One, two, three, four, five once I caught a fish alive

One, two, three, four, five
Once I caught a fish alive
Six, seven, eight, nine, ten
Then I let it go again
Why did you let it go?
Because it bit my finger so!
Which finger did it bite?
This little finger on my right.

Hello Joshua

Hel-lo Josh-u-a how are you to-day?
Hel-lo Josh-u-a what game shall we play?
(speaking) **How about** *(pause)* a tummy tickle
(say quickly and tickle)

Hop, skip and jump

With the children in a space of their own, choose form the following instructions and notice who can follow them and count correctly.
Jump four times!
Spin around three times.
Hop on one leg twice.
Take six steps.
Skip five times...etc

How many children?

(To the tune of Here we go round the mulberry bush)
In a small group select items of clothing, colour of hair or eyes, transport to setting or anything common to one or more of the group. Sing the rhyme then count the number of children it applies to. Include all the children in the first and last verse. For example:

How many children have jumpers today?
Jumpers today, jumpers today.
How many children have jumpers today?
Shall we count you?

Let's count to ten

(To the tune of London Bridge then chant numbers)
Boys and girls let's count to ten, count to ten, count to ten
Boys and girls let's count to ten
Are we ready?
One, two, three, four, five, six, seven, eight, nine, ten!

Peek-a-boo one, two, three

Play this game with up to three same or similar items. For example, Mr Bunny hops into view and tickles baby's tummy, hops out of sight then re-appears. Repeat a couple of times then two bunnies appear. Notice any changes in reaction and repeat. Alternate between one and two. When you are confident that the child is noticing the difference add a third.

Teddy bear, teddy bear

Teddy bear, teddy bear turn around,
Teddy bear, teddy bear, touch the ground
Teddy bear, teddy bear, curl up small
Teddy bear, teddy bear, stand up tall...
Teddy bear, teddy bear turn around,
Teddy bear, teddy bear, touch the ground
Teddy bear, teddy bear, switch off the light
Teddy bear, teddy bear, say goodnight!

Ready for bed

Make up counting rhymes to say at bedtime. For example, gather the child's favourite soft toys or teddies to put away at bedtime. As the first toy is put away say 'One toy ready for bed.' Then as the next toy joins it 'Two toys ready for bed.' Continue until all the toys are away and then finally count them all one more time and say goodnight to them.

Scrub-a-dub dub

Scrub-a-dub dub put *(insert child's name)* in the tub
And what do you think we should clean?
His fingers
His toesies
His little snub nosey
And everything else we see.

Ten green bottles

Ten green bottles hanging on the wall
Ten green bottles hanging on the wall
And if one green bottle should accidently fall
There'll be nine green bottles hanging on the wall...
(and so on until none!)

Twinkle, twinkle little shape

Twinkle, twinkle little square
One, two, three, four sides are there
Looking at the circle round
Will it roll along the ground?
Triangle your sides are three
Can you count them now with me?

Twinkle, twinkle little star
Stretch your arms and legs out far
Can you curl into a ball?
Like a sphere that's round and small
Stand up straight arms next to you
Like a rectangle, it's true!

When Goldilocks went to the house of the bears

When Goldilocks went to the house of the bears, oh what did her two eyes see?
A bowl that was huge, a bowl that was small, a bowl that was tiny and that was all,
She counted them: one, two, three.
Repeat for chair and bed, then
When Goldilocks ran from the house of the bears, oh what did her two eyes see?
A bear that was huge, a bear that was small, a bear that was tiny and that was all,
They growled at her: grrr, grrr, grrr!
You can also change Goldilocks to the child's name, checking the colour of their eyes with them in a mirror and adjusting the words accordingly.

Ten train trucks

Ten train trucks chuffing down the line,
One uncouples and now there are nine.
Nine train trucks running very late,
One breaks down and now there are eight.
Eight train trucks heading down to Devon
One needs a sleep and now there are seven
Seven train trucks driving, carrying lots of bricks
One crashes off and now there are six.
Six train trucks packed up ready for their drive
One forgets his lunch and now there are five

Five train trucks wishing there were more
Another uncouples and now there are four.
Four train trucks chuffing by the sea,
One stops at the beach, now there are three.
Three train trucks heading for the zoo
One feeds the animals and now there are two
Two train trucks looking for some fun
One spies a party and then there is one
One train truck chuffing down the line
Parks at the station and arrives on time.

2-D shape: also known as 2-dimensional. A shape that only has two dimensions (such as width and height) and no thickness.

3-D shape: also known as 3-dimensional. An object that has height, width and depth, like any object in the real world.

Abstract: something that exists as an idea or thought.

Addition: finding the total of two or more numbers.

Animated: lively and with action.

Assimilate: to take in and understand.

Attachments: the affectionate tie between the child and another person.

Calculation: a process involving addition, subtraction, multiplication or division that requires careful thought.

Capacity: the amount something can contain.

Cardinality: the number of elements or objects in a group or set.

Caretaker speech/parentese: a form of speech often used with babies. It can be higher in pitch than usual, has a sing-song quality and is often delivered with a smiling face, wide eyes and head movement.

Categorise: to put or sort things that have some similar or same features into a group.

Cause and effect: when something (the cause) makes something else happen (the effect).

Commentating: speaking out loud about what you notice the child doing whilst you play alongside them. This provides them with new vocabulary and models correct speech.

Concrete: something real that exists in a physical form.

Continuous counting: counting measures in order to find out how much, how heavy or how long things are.

Currency: a country's money system.

Decrease: to become smaller or fewer in amount or size.

Digit: any one of the Arabic numerals 1 to 9 and the symbol 0.

Direct modelling: using actual objects to represent a problem physically e.g. real pieces of fruit or real biscuits.

Discrete counting: counting things using numbers in order to find out how many there are.

Estimate: an informed guess at how many or how much.

Fine motor: movements that require a high degree of control and precision. These may include drawing, writing, cutting with scissors, using cutlery.

Hand-eye coordination: ability to use the eyes and hands together to perform an activity, for example, stringing beads, completing puzzles, playing board games.

Heuristic play: play that allows children to initiate, make choices, explore and discover the properties ar qualities of objects.

Increase: to become greater or larger in amount or size.

Internalise: absorb learning at a deeper level.

Mass: how much matter is in an object, which is measured in grams and kilograms.

Mathematical graphics: the marks and representations used by children to express their mathematical thoughts. The child chooses how to represent their ideas in a way that is meaningful to them.

Minuend: the first (and usually largest) number in a subtraction.

Moveable objects: a range of small objects that are easy to move and manipulate.

Multi-sensory exploration: using one or more sens to explore and begin to make sense of the world around them.

Non-measuring reasoning: comparing objects by looking at their size in relation to each other.

Number sense: the child's inner understanding of numbers, what they mean and their relationship to on another including within a problem.

Numeral: a word or symbol used to represent a digit

Object permanence: understanding that things continue to exist even when they cannot be seen, heard, touched, smelt or sensed.

One-to-one correspondence: being able to point to an individual object while counting and saying the correct numeral (touch counting).

Open ended/possibility questions: questions that can't be answered with one or two words. They generally require more thoughtful responses. Open ended questions usually begin with who, why, what, how or I wonder.

Pattern: a repeated sequence or design.

Positional language: words that describe where an object is in relation to other objects.

Prime carer: the person the child spends most time with e.g. parent at home or key person in a setting.

Quantity: how many things there are or how much there is.

pertoire: a stock of words, songs and rhymes that regularly used.

te learning: memorising facts through repetition.

affold: support given to help move a child to the xt level of learning.

hema: a repeated pattern of behaviour which pports a child in their exploration and understanding heir world. These may include; grasping, sitioning, transporting and enclosing.

ribe: to write a child's words as they are spoken.

t: a group or collection of objects or numbers that ve something in common.

atial awareness: the recognition of the distance ween objects and the ability to judge where you are elation to objects.

ble order: knowing that numbers are always said he same order.

bitise: the ability to recognize the number of objects set without counting.

btraction: taking one number away from another.

btrahend: the number that is taken away.

m: the total of two or more amounts.

mmative: an end assessment of a child's learning development.

ly: a score used for counting. It is common to tally g straight lines. Once children start to count in fives four vertical lines and one diagonal line to represent roup of five.

tal: the whole number or amount.

nsitivity: knowing that an object is longer or shorter n another through direct comparison with a third ect.

lue: how much something is worth.

ual acuity: the clarity with which we see details and pes of objects.

ual discrimination: distinguishing similarities and erences between shapes and objects.

lume: the amount of space filled by an object or stance, or the amount of space inside a container.

Useful vocabulary

(From *Mathematical Vocabulary* The National Numeracy Strategy Dec 2000)

Position, direction and movement: over, under, above, below, top, bottom, side, on, in, outside, inside, around, in front, behind, front, back, before, after, beside, next to, opposite, apart, between, middle, edge, corner, direction, left, right, up, down, forwards, backwards, sideways, across, close, far, near, along, through, to, from, towards, away from, movement, slide, roll, turn, stretch, bend.

Exploring patterns, shape and space: shape, pattern, flat, curved, straight, round, hollow, solid, corner, face, side, edge, end, sort, make, build, draw.

3D shapes: cube, pyramid, sphere, cone.

2D shapes: circle, triangle, square, rectangle, star.

Patterns and symmetry: size, bigger, larger, smaller, symmetrical pattern, repeating pattern, match.

Measures (general): measure, size, compare, guess, estimate, enough, not enough, too much, too little, too many, too few, nearly, close to, about the same as, just over, just under.

Length: length, width, height, depth, long, short, tall, high, low, wide, narrow, deep, shallow, thick, thin longer, shorter, taller, higher… and so on longest, shortest, tallest, highest… and so on far, near, close.

Mass: weigh, weighs, balances, heavy/light, heavier/lighter, heaviest/lightest, balance, scales, weight.

Capacity: full, half full, empty, holds, container.

Time: time, days of the week: Monday, Tuesday… day, week, birthday, holiday, morning, afternoon, evening, night, bedtime, dinnertime, playtime today, yesterday, tomorrow, before, after next, last, now, soon, early, late, quick, quicker, quickest, quickly, slow, slower, slowest, slowly, old, older, oldest, new, newer, newest, takes longer, takes less time, hour, o'clock, clock, watch, hands.

Money: compare, double, half, halve, pair, count out, share out, left, left over, money, coin, penny, pence, pound, price, cost, buy, sell, spend, spent, pay, change, dear, costs more, cheap, costs less, cheaper, costs the same as, how much…? how many…? total.

Articles/publications

Statutory Framework for the Early Years:
www.gov.uk/government/publications/eyfsframework

Development Matters: www.early-education.org.uk

Barwell, R (contributing author). *The role of language in mathematics*. Reading: National Association for Language Development in the Curriculum.

Copley, J V. (2009) The Young Child and Mathematics (2nd Ed.). Washington DC: The National Association for the Education of Young Children.

Children Thinking Mathematically: PSRN essential knowledge for Early Years practitioners The National Strategies 2009

Geist, E. (2009) *Children are Born Mathematicians: Supporting Mathematical Development, Birth to Age Eight*. New York: Pearson.

Greeno, G. Riley, M S. Gelman, R. (1984) *Conceptual Competence and Children's Counting*. Pittsburg: Academic Press

Holton, D. (1999) *Teaching Problem Solving*. Chichester: Kingsham Press

Learning Trajectories in Mathematics CPRE (Consortium for Policy Research in Education) January 2011

NCETM (National Centre for Excellence in the Teaching of Mathematics) Early Years Magazine Issue 7

Skinner, C (2011). *Maths is Everywhere*. London: The British Association for Early Childhood Education.

Taylor, H. (2013) *How Children Learn Mathematics and the Implications for Teaching: Chapter 1*. London: Sage.

Way, J. (2005) *Number Sense Series: Developing Early Number Sense*. NRICH.

Websites

www.mathsisfun.com

http://www.slideshare.net/mflaming/developing-number-concepts-in-k2-learners

www.foundationyears.org.uk *Follow link to Nationa Strategies Resources Library.*

http://mathsolutions.com/making-sense-of-math/number-sense/understanding-number-sense/

http://www.teachingintheearlyyears.com/2011/11/mental-math-subtraction-strategies.html